OVERCOMERS' GUIDE TO THE KINGDOM

Another Perspective of The Sermon on the Mount

James T. Harman

Prophecy
Countdown
Publications

OVERCOMERS' GUIDE TO THE KINGDOM

Copyright © 2011, James T. Harman

Prophecy Countdown Publications, LLC
P.O. Box 941612
Maitland, FL 32794
www.ProphecyCountdown.com

ISBN: 978-0-9636984-4-5

All references from Scripture are from the King James Version unless noted otherwise: Wuest New Testament, copyright © 1961 Eerdmans Publishing
ESV – English Standard Version®, copyright © 2001 Crossway
NLT – New Living Translation, copyright © 1996
NIV – New International Version, copyright © 1973
NKJV- New King James Version, copyright © 1982
by Thomas Nelson, Inc. Used by permission.

Words in bold emphasis are authors and not in original Scripture.

Numerical references to selected words in the text of Scripture are from James H. Strong Dictionaries of the Hebrew and Greek words.

Certain words such as Kingdom and Judgement Seat are capitalized to emphasize their importance, but not in accordance with Traditional fashion.

Credit and Copyright for pictures inside this book:
Page 72 – Bride with veil (#504) courtesy of: www.EricaKoesler.com

---

The enhanced pictures on the front and back covers are rare images of The Mount of Beatitudes. They are color photochrome prints taken between 1890 & 1900 in Capernaum, Israel. Similar prints may be viewed at: www.loc.gov
The beautiful lilies on the back cover are courtesy of: www.treesflowers.com

Excerpt of What Readers Are Saying

"I believe this is the best book that Jim has written, and it covers a topic that is vital for every Christian who wants to be found faithful at the Judgment Seat of Christ."
Lyn Mize – Ooltewah, TN
First Fruits Ministry

"This writing presents a notable challenge to the body of Christ to come to terms with the sanctification process as you have related it." Karen Bishop – Glasgow, KY

"Jim always does a beautiful job in explaining the importance of our role as overcomers in Christ. I especially love the comparisons between the Beatitudes in Matthew with "the fruit of the Spirit" in Galatians." Robin J. Wade – Ft. Pierce, FL

*"Thank you for your new book: **Overcomers' Guide to the Kingdom.** Lots of new ideas and skillfully written."*
Nancy Missler – Coeur d'Alene, ID
The Kings Highway Ministries

"I commend your presentation of the Kingdom aspect of the Lord's message on the mountain, and that it is offering us so much more than mere salvation from sins or entrance into heaven." Wayne Smith – Grove City, OH
Living Walk Journal

"I believe your book will greatly assist others in their journey toward the coming Kingdom as it relates the standards that will come to bear with Christians as they face our Lord at His Judgment Seat." Charles F. Strong – Harlingen, TX
Bible One Ministry

"James Harman has done an amazing job in presenting a fresh and challenging look at the timeless words of Jesus found in "The Sermon on the Mount." In a day of shallow commitment and easy believism, the words of Jesus again ring true for those who would find their inheritance as genuine overcomers..."

Pastor Tom Myers – Longwood, FL
Neighborhood Alliance Church

"Thank you for your new book: **Overcomers' Guide to the Kingdom**. *It is refreshing to see people awakening to the truths of accountability...I am sincerely thankful for your insight into these issues. I pray more would awake to see these things and make sure they understand the Lord's judgments – for in these days, it just may be that it will make the difference between a person enduring...or not."*

Pastor Joey Faust – Venus, TX
Author of **The Rod-Will God Spare It?**

"This book is the "crown jewel" of all of Jim's writings...and is written in the common man's language that even a child can understand. May all who read it be numbered among those to hear: "Well done good and faithful servant...enter into MY Joy."
Joan Olsen – Edmond, OK

The complete comments by the above readers begin on Page 90.

Prologue

The Sermon on the Mount is one of the most important sermons that Jesus ever gave. Our Lord had already been baptized in the Jordan River, tempted by the devil in the desert, and started His ministry of preaching to the Gentiles in the area of the sea of Galilee. He had called His first disciples who immediately left their previous way of life to follow Him. Jesus spent time teaching in the synagogues and preaching the good news about the Kingdom. At this time, He also was actively healing the people of every disease and sickness. News about this spread, and **great multitudes** of people came to hear Him speak and to be healed of their infirmities.

With this as a backdrop, Matthew begins this great Sermon:

> *"And seeing the multitudes, He **went up on a mountain**, and when He was seated His **disciples** came to Him."* (Matthew 5:1 – NKJV)

It is important to notice that Jesus left the great multitudes of people and climbed up on a mountain to give this important Sermon. Also, please notice that the disciples were the main audience for this essential teaching. These observations are vital in understanding the true meaning of this Sermon.

Hundreds of books have been written on Chapters 5-7 of the gospel of Matthew. Interpretations of this Sermon vary widely; and while some authors understand its true significance, I am not aware of any books that have taken the perspective that this short work will attempt to do.

Two years ago, I wrote my most important book dealing with what's in store for the Church. It is called: *THE KINGDOM* and it is available for free download from our website located at: www.ProphecyCountdown.com

Readers are highly encouraged to download and read *THE KINGDOM* before you read this current book. Pay particular attention to Chapters 10 and 11, which deal with what it means to be an overcomer and entering into the coming Kingdom.

This current work is really a sequel to *THE KINGDOM*. Sensing the need to provide further assistance for Christians to properly prepare for what lies ahead, this book was started. As I began my own climb up the mountain, the Lord graciously reminded me that I need the instructions in this book as much as anyone else! While preparing to write this manuscript, I was confronted with a most astounding personal revelation:

> *"Therefore everyone who is of such character as to be **habitually hearing** these words of mine and **habitually doing them**, shall be likened to an intelligent man who is of such a nature that he built his house upon the rocky cliff."* (Matthew 7:25 – Wuest New Testament)

Being totally honest with myself, I had to admit that I have not been habitually reading and hearing the words of my Lord in this important Sermon. While I have been a disciple of Jesus Christ for several decades, have written numerous books on eschatology, and have always tried to follow the Lord in all that I do; I was taken aback by the words: ***habitually doing them***.

So while this book was originally intended to help Christians prepare for the coming Kingdom, the Lord showed me that I need this book as much as anyone else.

The Sermon on the Mount was delivered by our Lord to teach His disciples what their new life was to be like. If you are a Christian today, are you also a disciple? Are you habitually hearing and doing the things Jesus tells you to do in this short Sermon? The purpose of this book is to help you be the overcomer Jesus wants you to be and to help you gain your own entrance in the coming Kingdom.

Dedication

This book is dedicated to the thirsty and hungry believer who senses that something might not be quite right in their Christian walk. May this short work help guide you on the narrow path that few care to follow.

> *"28) Come to Me, all you who labor and are heavy laden, and I will give you rest. 29) Take My yoke upon you and learn from Me, for I am gentle and lowly in heart, and you will find rest for your souls. 30) For My yoke is easy and My burden is light."*
> (Matthew 11:28-30 – NKJV)

―――――――――――――――――――――

"Christ preached this Sermon, which was an exposition of the Law, upon a mountain, because upon a mountain the Law was given: and this was also a solemn promulgation of the Christian Law. But observe the difference: when the Law was given the Lord came down upon the mountain, now the Lord 'went up' into one; then He spoke in thunder and lightning, now in a still small voice; then the people were ordered to keep their distance, now they are invited to draw near – a blessed change!" (Matthew Henry – 1662 to 1714)

FOREWARNING ABOUT CONTENTS

If either Jesus or John the Baptist appeared today with a manuscript of their material, how many publishers do you think they would have to visit before they found one willing to carry their harsh messages?

> *"Woe to you, teachers of the law and Pharisees, you hypocrites! You shut the kingdom of heaven in men's faces. You yourselves do not enter, nor will you let those enter who are trying to."*
> (Matthew 23:13 – NIV)

> *"..Repent ye: for the kingdom of heaven is at hand. For this is he that was spoken of... one crying in the wilderness, Prepare ye the way of the Lord, make his paths straight."*   (Matthew 3:2-3)

The many Christian publishing houses across our land would be hesitant to take on such a new title that would not be popularly received by the mainstream Church. Seeing that they couldn't make a sufficient profit with their messages, they would probably have to send them on their way.

OVERCOMERS' GUIDE TO THE KINGDOM was written to help people realize the Lord's famous Sermon may have some important precepts that have been overlooked by many. While you probably did not find this book in your local Christian bookstore, be prepared to experience a paradigm shift in some of your Christian beliefs.

Table of Contents

Matthew – Chapter 4

"From this time Jesus began to PREACH and to SAY, 'REPENT, for the KINGDOM of Heaven is at hand...and He said to them, follow me, and I will make you fishers of men...now Jesus went about all Galilee....preaching the Gospel of the KINGDOM..." (Matthew 4:17-23)

Foreword

James Harman's previous work, *THE KINGDOM* as well as this sequel, *OVERCOMERS' GUIDE TO THE KINGDOM* contain what must be viewed as the missing ingredient to what Scripture presents as "the gospel" namely, the message of the Kingdom of God. The often used phrase, "the gospel" actually means "good news." What is widely presented today under the banner of "the gospel" is the isolated message of the need to be born again. What is not widely presented along with the vital need to be born again is the good news of the coming of the Kingdom of God as a real and viable alternative to living under the influence of the kingdoms of this present world. In stating that *"My Kingdom is not of this world"* (John 18:36), Jesus makes a clear declaration that His Kingdom is in direct opposition to all present earthly kingdoms, including the one in which we presently live, America. No earthly kingdom has ever been, or will ever be prior to the return of Christ, a manifestation of the Kingdom of God. This was the error of the zealous Puritans in proclaiming that America was founded to be a geographical manifestation of the Kingdom of God on earth:

"In the Virgin Wilderness of America, God was making His most significant attempt since ancient Israel to create a New Israel of people living in obedience to the law of God...The Puritans understood New England to be...a New Jerusalem, a model of Christ upon the Earth – A model of the Kingdom of Christ upon the Earth – We Americans were intended to be living proof to the rest of the world..."
(pages 22-23,*"The Light & the Glory"* by Peter Marshall)

It is my firm conviction that the present thrust of politically-minded Christians to dominate this country is the product of such erroneous Puritan theology. We Christians are not on this earth to dominate its unregenerate inhabitants, but rather to influence them with the real "good news" of the gospel that Jesus preached (please see: Matthew 4:17-23 on facing page).

-11-

The good news we are to preach includes the Kingdom. It is important to see that the exhortation Jesus makes in Matthew 4 is a precursor that leads right into rest of the message about the Kingdom of God; the contents of which this book you are about to read is all about. It is a message every born-again Christian needs to continue to meditate upon: how to live in the spiritual Kingdom of God while dwelling in a physical kingdom of this world that is under the sway of the Wicked One (1 Jn. 5:18-19).

Today's gospel is devoid of the dual emphasis Jesus placed on (1) the need to *"Repent"* and (2) *"The Kingdom of Heaven"* being at hand. The gospel has been diminished to the isolated message of *"the new birth."* The message of life in the Kingdom of God as depicted in Chapters 5-7 of the gospel of Matthew is about *"the new life"* that God's people are now called to live.

Most teachings I have heard about "the Sermon on the Mount" are an erroneous doctrinal pendulum swing as either being (1) a message to those who were under the dispensation of Old Covenant Law, or (2) are projected as instruction for saints living in the future dispensation of the Millennial Reign of Christ on earth. Neither of these positions are true! The contents of the Sermon on the Mount are for New Covenant born-again believers like you and me!

It is quite significant to me that it is within the confines of the Sermon on the Mount that Jesus, the King of the Kingdom, presents the pathway to the Kingdom as being obtained only by entering a narrow gate – with a difficult way – in order to walk on the other side of that gate (see Matthew 7:13-14).

It is the call to repentance that makes the gate narrow. Obeying the multitude of newly defined laws and principles contained within the Sermon on the Mount will make for the Christian walk to be a difficult and costly way to live as a follower of Christ.

Pastor Randy Shupe
The Way, the Truth and the Life Tabernacle

-12-

Preface

Moses came down a mountain to give God's laws written in stone. The Ten Commandments represent the laws of God as given to Moses to communicate requirements for people to keep.

Jesus went up a mountain to give believers His new laws to be written on their hearts. This was a fulfillment of the following:

> *"I will raise up for them a Prophet like you from among their brethren, and will put My words in His mouth, and He shall speak to them all that I command Him."* (Deuteronomy 18:18 – NKJV)

Through Jesus, God has once again communicated new laws which He wants people to follow.

Many Christians will immediately protest and object, and say that we are not under the law, but under grace. Yes, it is true that under the New Covenant we are saved by grace:

> *"For by grace are ye saved through faith; and that not of yourselves: it is the gift of God: Not of works, lest any man should boast."* (Ephesians 2:8-9)

However, Jesus did not come to abolish the law, but to fulfill it:

> *"Do not think that I came to destroy the Law or the Prophets. I did not come to destroy but to fulfill."* (Matthew 5:17 – NKJV)

The Apostle Paul refers to this new law when he said:

> *"Bear ye one another's burdens, and so fulfill the **law of Christ.**"* (Galatians 6:2)

Here the Apostle Paul was referring to the New Testament law that Jesus gave in His Sermon on the Mount. This entire sermon represents Christ's teachings (*law of Christ*) that need to be followed for the believer to gain their own entrance into the coming Kingdom.

Remember how Jesus said the whole Law and the Prophets can be summed up:

> *"36) 'Teacher, which is the great commandment in the law?' 37) Jesus said to him, 'You shall love the LORD your God with all your heart, with all your soul, and with all your mind.' 38) 'This is the first and great commandment. 39) And the second is like it: 'You shall love your neighbor as yourself.' 40) On these two commandments hang all the Law and the Prophets."* (Matthew 22:36-40)

Both Paul and James echo Christ's words:

> *"For all the law is fulfilled in one word, even in this: 'You shall love your neighbor as yourself."* (Galatians 5:14 – NKJV)

> *"If you really fulfill the royal law according to the Scripture, You shall love your neighbor as yourself, you do well;"* (James 2:8 – NKJV)

Jesus, Paul and James all agree that love is the key to fulfillment of all the law. God gives mankind laws because He loves us. He wants what is best for us and gives us guidelines to follow for our own good. The Sermon that is discussed in the following pages represents guidelines believers should be habitually hearing and habitually doing as we approach the soon return of our Lord.

> *"If you love Me, keep My commandments."* (John 14:15 – NKJV)

Chapter 1 – Overcomers' Characteristics

Jesus begins His sermon in a most curious way. Remember, this Sermon is addressed to His disciples:

> *"1) And seeing the multitudes, He went up on a mountain, and when He was seated **His disciples came to Him**. 2) Then He opened His mouth and taught them, saying:"* (Matthew 5:1-2 – NKJV)

Jesus then begins by teaching His disciples about 9 qualities and characteristics that they should either possess now or strive for in their walk with Him. Had the great multitudes made the steep climb up the mountain, they would have heard a Sermon that would not have made any sense to them. But those He was addressing were His disciples who had already made the decision to follow Jesus up the mountain. They were committed believers who wanted to hear His teachings.

It is critical to understand that being a committed follower of Jesus Christ is a prerequisite for ever meeting the requirements of these new *"laws of Christ."* In other words, being born again is the necessary qualification to even be able to hear and understand these new laws. To the natural man, these new requirements are impossible. Only those who have been given a new Spirit from above will be in a position to comprehend what Jesus is saying and only by allowing the Holy Spirit to control their life will they be the overcomers that God will bless.

It is also important to point out that people are not made good by doing good. First a person needs a new heart (i.e., be born-again), and then good works will follow:

> *"For by grace are ye saved through faith; and that not of yourselves: it is the gift of God: Not of works, lest any man should boast. **For we are his workmanship created in Christ Jesus unto good works.**"* (Ephesians 2:8-10)

In other words, the good works Jesus wants to see represents the fruit of the Spirit that is evidence of a life that is truly led by the Holy Spirit.

Interestingly, Jesus lists 9 Beatitudes in His Sermon on the Mount and the Apostle Paul also lists 9 Fruits of the Spirit:

> *"22) But the fruit of the Spirit is love, joy, peace, longsuffering (patience), gentleness (kindness), goodness, faith, 23) Meekness, temperance (self-control): against such there is no law."* (Galatians 5:22-23)

Let's look at each of the 9 Beatitudes which describe the essential characteristics every disciple should possess.

The Poor in Spirit

> *"Blessed are the poor in spirit, For theirs is the kingdom of heaven."* (Matthew 5:3 – NKJV)

The first step in becoming a Christian is recognizing our need for a Saviour. Jesus begins His listing of 9 Beatitudes with the foundation that is necessary for all of the remaining qualities. If a person never comes to realize that they are in need of a Saviour, then the rest of this Sermon will not make any sense to them.

The first quality of a new Christian is realizing just how helpless we are without Jesus. The Greek word for **poor** (#4434) in this verse means: *destitute or powerless*. When we come to the place in our life where we realize we are absolutely nothing on our own and that we need to place our life in God's hands, we then enter into that Blessed state where Jesus saves us. By taking this initial step of humbly recognizing our need, the Lord blesses us with an inheritance in the Kingdom.

The first step in being an overcomer, is placing our faith in Jesus:

> *"4) For whatsoever is born of God overcometh the world: and this is the victory that overcometh the world, even **our faith**. 5) Who is he that overcometh the world, but he that believeth that Jesus is the Son of God?"*
> (I John 5:4-5)

The first two times the word *"overcometh"* is used is found in the above Scripture. John is telling us that only those who are born of God, and believe that Jesus is the Son of God, have overcome the world by their faith. All that is required to overcome the world is the Christian's faith in Jesus Christ. While accepting Christ is vital to becoming an overcomer, it is really only the first step. In order to be a successful overcomer, the Christian also must be able to overcome the flesh and overcome the devil. Only when all three are defeated (the world, the flesh and the devil), will the Christian be considered a true overcomer.

As mentioned earlier, there are 9 Beatitudes listed in the Sermon on the Mount and 9 Fruits of the Spirit. This does not appear to be merely a coincidence because there appears to be a striking connection between the two lists.

The first Beatitude is recognizing our spiritual poverty and coming to the Lord in faith. But remember, even this faith is a gift from God (Ephesians 2:8-9), and one of the 9 Fruits of the Spirit is *faith*. The overcomer begins his journey with Christ with the essential fruit of the Spirit: *"even our faith."*

Those Who Mourn

> *"Blessed are those who mourn, For they shall be comforted."* (Matthew 5:4 – NKJV)

The next step in being a successful overcomer is recognizing how spiritually wretched we really are. One of the keys to being able to overcome the flesh and the devil is to realize our need to seek God's help. Every sin that we commit should lead us to God for help:

> *"O wretched man that I am! Who will deliver me from this body of death?"* (Romans 7:24)

The overcoming Christian will feel deep sorrow every time that they sin. The closer one walks with the Lord, the more sin becomes an affront to our relationship. Fortunately, this Beatitude ends with the promise: *For they shall be comforted.*

The person who is sorry for his sins will regularly confess them to God and receive the comfort of knowing that his sins are forgiven:

> *"If we confess our sins, he is faithful and just to forgive us our sins, and to cleanse us from all unrighteousness."* (I John 1:9)

The Fruit of the Spirit that most directly relates to this Beatitude is the fruit of: **goodness**. The Greek word for goodness (#19) is: *uprightness of heart and life.* The overcoming Christian who mourns over his sins truly possesses an uprightness of heart and has the desire to draw closer to the Lord.

The Meek

> *"Blessed are the meek, For they shall inherit the earth."* (Matthew 5:5 – NKJV)

The third Beatitude Jesus mentions is the characteristic of meekness. To be meek is to be submissive to the Lord in whatever circumstance we may find ourselves in. Meekness is not weakness, but a humble reliance upon God. To be meek is the opposite of being self-assertive. Through the circumstances that life brings, the overcomer learns to trust in God's goodness to control.

While the natural man is full of pride, self-interest and self-assertiveness; the overcomer, being led by the Holy Spirit, will produce the fruit of: *meekness* which will be evidenced by a gentle and mild spirit.

The blessing associated with this attribute is the inheritance of the earth which was also alluded to by David:

> *"But the meek shall inherit the earth; and shall delight themselves in the abundance of peace."* (Psalm 37:11)

The meek learn to submit their entire life to the will of God, and will be greatly blessed by inheriting the earth.

Those Who Hunger & Thirst For Righteousness

> *"Blessed are those who hunger and thirst for righteousness, For they shall be filled."*
> (Matthew 5:6 – NKJV)

The fourth Beatitude deals with the righteousness of the believer.   When we are saved, we receive the imputed righteousness of Jesus (Isaiah 61:10).   All believers receive Christ's righteousness upon our salvation. After we are saved, the overcomer continues to hunger and thirst for righteousness by seeking Him through His word.

> *"And Jesus said to them, 'I am the bread of life. He who comes to Me shall never hunger, and he who believes in Me shall never thirst."* (John 6:35 – NKJV)

The overcomer should continue to hunger and thirst for more and more of Jesus every day. Those who do, are given the wonderful promise that they will be filled.

The Fruit of the Spirit related to this Beatitude is the fruit of: *love*. The overcoming Christian, who truly seeks the righteousness of God on a daily basis, is filled with a love toward God that is indeed a blessing. Spending time with the Lord can be one of the greatest blessings in this life.

The Merciful

> *"Blessed are the merciful, For they shall obtain mercy."*
> (Matthew 5:7 – NKJV)

The fifth attribute of the overcomer is mercy. The Greek word for mercy #1655 (eleēmōn) appears only twice. Here in Matthew 5:7 and also in Hebrews 2:17:

> *"For this reason he had to be made like his brothers in every way, in order that he might become a **merciful** and faithful high priest in service to God, and that he might make atonement for the sins of the people."*
> (Hebrews 2:17 – NIV)

Oh what a wonderful Lord we serve! To think that He left heaven to be made *"like His brothers"* i.e., like us, so he could be a **merciful** High Priest.

Because we have been shown such mercy by God, the overcomer is filled with compassion towards his fellow man. Having been the recipient of such marvelous grace, the believer is compelled to act graciously towards others.

The blessing to be derived for those who have been merciful is to obtain mercy at the coming Judgement Seat of Christ. The following verse shows why the overcomer should extend mercy towards others:

"For judgment is without mercy to the one who has shown no mercy. Mercy triumphs over judgment." (James 2:13 – NKJV)

The above verse reveals the more merciful we have been, the more mercy the Lord will show us at the coming Judgement Seat.

The Fruit of the Spirit related to the Beatitude of mercy is the fruit of: *kindness.* The overcomer, being led by the Spirit of God is moved with compassion and kindness in his dealings with others.

The Pure in Heart

"Blessed are the pure in heart, For they shall see God." (Matthew 5:8 – NKJV)

The sixth characteristic of the overcomer is to be pure in heart. The Greek word for pure #2513 (katharos) has several different aspects to it. In the physical realm it relates to being purified by fire as with gold and silver so as to remove any impurities, or to the pruning of a tree in order that it may bear more fruit. It is also used to describe someone who is free from any corrupt desire, free from sin and guilt, or free from any falsity. It is also used to describe a person who is innocent, blameless, and not guilty of anything.

To attain to the level of purity God desires is impossible for the flesh to reach, however through the help of the Holy Spirit, the overcomer is constantly learning how to crucify the old flesh nature and dying to self. By relying on God's help, the overcomer can walk the holy, blameless path of purity that will one day allow them to see God:

*"3) Who may ascend into the **hill of the LORD**? Or who may stand in His holy place? 4) He who has clean*

*hands and a **pure heart**, Who has not lifted up his soul to an idol, Nor sworn deceitfully. 5) He shall receive blessing from the LORD, And righteousness from the God of his salvation.* " (Psalm 24:3-5 – NKJV)

The promised blessing for those who have a pure heart will be to see God in the coming Kingdom (***hill of the Lord***). This truth was also alluded to in John's first letter:

*"2) Beloved, now we are children of God; and it has not yet been revealed what we shall be, but we know that when He is revealed, we shall be like Him, **for we shall see Him as He is. 3) And everyone who has this hope in Him purifies himself, just as He is pure.**"*
(I John 3:2-3 – NKJV)

In order to obtain this wonderful blessing, the overcomers' life will produce the fruit of: *self-control*. Every day, the believer will be confronted by the world, the flesh and the devil. The successful overcomer will learn to seek God's help to obtain the required self-control. By continually reading God's word and asking for the Holy Spirit's help, the believer will attain the crucial victory.

The Peacemakers

"Blessed are the peacemakers, For they shall be called sons of God." (Matthew 5:9 – NKJV)

The first six Beatitudes dealt either with inward attributes or characteristics relating to our upward relationship with God. The final three Beatitudes will concentrate on our outward relationships with others. To be a peacemaker, one must first be at peace with himself and with God.

"Great peace have those who love Your law, And nothing causes them to stumble."
(Psalm 119:165 – NKJV)

The true source of the overcomers' peace can only come from his relationship with God and a love of His word. As the Psalmist indicates, nothing can make one stumble who loves God's law.

After the overcomer has matured in his own faith, he will then be in a position to attempt to pursue peace with others.

> *"Pursue peace with all people, and holiness, without which no one will see the Lord..."*
> (Hebrews 12:14 – NKJV)

The pursuit of peace with all people seems only natural for a mature disciple of Christ, because Jesus is known as the Prince of Peace (Isaiah 9:6). As His subjects in the coming Kingdom, the peacemakers will receive the promise of being called sons of God as this Beatitude assures us. The promises to peacemakers are also confirmed by James when he wrote:

> *"Peacemakers who sow in peace raise a harvest of righteousness."* (James 3:18 – NIV)

Of course the Fruit of the Spirit related to the Beatitude of the Peacemaker is the fruit of: *peace.* The mature overcomer knows the peace of God in his own life and he wants to spread this wonderful quality to others:

> *"Therefore let us pursue the things which make for peace and the things by which one may edify another."*
> (Romans 14:19 – NKJV)

Those Persecuted for Righteousness

> *"Blessed are those who are persecuted for righteousness' sake, For theirs is the kingdom of heaven."* (Matthew 5:10 – NKJV)

The eighth Beatitude shows why being a true overcomer is not the easy road to follow. The overcomers' allegiance is to their

Master, and while living in this fallen world is not easy, they have determined to stand up for Christ no matter what the cost. The Apostle Paul confirms this in his second letter to Timothy:

> *"Yes, and all who desire to live godly in Christ Jesus will suffer persecution."* (II Timothy 3:12 – NKJV)

The Christian who is an overcomer has exhibited the qualities and attributes described in the previous Beatitudes and purposed to live a Godly, holy life controlled by the Holy Spirit. The world and even much of the current lukewarm Church despises the Godly characteristics exhibited by these overcomers because they are convicted by their own carnal lifestyles. As a result, the true overcomer suffers persecution and is ostracized for their Godly behavior and stand for righteousness.

The wonderful promise associated with this persecution is their inheritance in the coming Kingdom:

> *"11) This is a faithful saying: For if we died with Him, We shall also live with Him. 12) If we endure, We shall also reign with Him..."* (II Timothy 2:11-12 – NKJV)

The successful overcomer is given the magnificent promise of reigning with Christ in His coming Kingdom!

The Fruit of the Spirit related to the Beatitude of Persecution for Righteousness is the fruit of: *patience*. The overcomer who has learned to suffer persecution for righteousness is given the fruit of patient endurance while in this world.

The Reviled and Persecuted

> *"11) Blessed are you when they revile and persecute you, and say all kinds of evil against you falsely for My sake. 12) Rejoice and be exceedingly glad, for great is your reward in heaven, for so they persecuted the prophets who were before you."*
> (Matthew 5:11-12 – NKJV)

In the final characteristic Jesus addresses the disciple personally (notice: "you" as opposed to "those"). This is probably because the persecution described here goes a step further. Jesus says, *"when they revile"* you. The Greek word for *"revile"* #3769, (oneidizō) means: *"of undeserved reproach."*

Here, the overcomer is faced with underserved reproach and persecution just because they are standing up for Christ. This type of persecution can come from the world and even today's lukewarm Laodicean Church. The mature overcomer is following in their Lord's footsteps:

> *"21) For to this you were called, because Christ also suffered for us, leaving us an example, that you should follow His steps: 22) Who committed no sin, Nor was deceit found in His mouth; 23) who, **when He was reviled**, did not revile in return; when He suffered, He did not threaten, but committed Himself to Him who judges righteously..."* (I Peter 2:21-23 – NKJV)

Jesus tells the disciple that they should *"rejoice and be exceedingly glad, for great is your reward in heaven."* While today's suffering may be hard and unpleasant to endure, the successful overcomer will identify with Paul:

> *"For I consider that the sufferings of this present time are not worthy to be compared with the glory which shall be revealed in us."* (Romans 8:18 – NKJV)

While this future glory is only partially understood, the Fruit of the Spirit the overcomer has experienced in this age is the fruit of: *joy.* But the joy felt now is only a foretaste of the joy to come when the overcomer is granted entrance into the coming Kingdom with these words:

> *"Well done, good and faithful servant...Enter into the joy of your lord."* (Matthew 25:21 – NKJV)

Comparison of Beatitudes with Fruit of the Spirit

Beatitude	Blessing	Fruit
1 Poor in Spirit	Theirs is the Kingdom	Faith
2 They that Mourn	They shall be Comforted	Goodness
3 The Meek	They shall inherit the Earth	Meekness
4 Hunger & Thirst for Righteousness	They shall be Filled	Love
5 Merciful	They shall obtain Mercy	Kindness
6 Pure in Heart	They shall see God	Self-Control
7 Peacemaker	They shall be Sons of God	Peace
8 Persecuted for Righteousness	Theirs is the Kingdom	Patience
9 Reviled & Persecuted	Great is your Reward	Joy

Chapter 2 – Overcomers' Influence

After describing the qualities and characteristics that the believer should exhibit in order to be a blessed overcomer, the Lord goes on to describe the influence they should have on this world:

Salt of the Earth

> *"You are the salt of the earth; but if the salt loses its flavor, how shall it be seasoned? It is then good for nothing but to be thrown out and trampled underfoot by men."* (Matthew 5:13 – NKJV)

The first similarity Jesus uses to illustrate the influence the disciple should display is that of salt. Salt was a precious commodity at the time of Christ. Salt was the primary means used to preserve food that would otherwise have been completely spoiled. The main characteristic of salt is its ability to act as a preservative and to prevent decay.

In a similar manner, Christ is revealing to His disciples that their main function will be to preserve wholesomeness in the earth and to arrest the spread of sin and corruption. Another interesting quality of salt is that it can make a person thirsty. In a comparable manner, the overcomer should generate a desire in others to thirst for the *"living water"* that only Christ can provide (John 7:38). Remember, Jesus had just enumerated the many characteristics that the successful overcomer should possess. Because his disciples are called to be His ambassadors, their lives should radiate Jesus – creating a yearning to be filled with this same living water.

However, in the last part of Matthew 5:13 notice that Jesus alludes to the salt losing its effectiveness. This is a picture of the Christian losing the essential qualities and characteristics that had just been discussed. Jesus is warning His disciples that it is possible for the salt to lose its flavor. This is a picture of the believer who is no longer exhibiting the characteristics of an overcomer because they have turned back to following their old flesh nature instead of being filled with the Spirit. They are portrayed by the lukewarm Church of Laodicea:

> *"I am rich, have become wealthy, and have need of nothing'—and do not know that you are wretched, miserable, poor, blind, and naked.."* (Rev.3:17 – NKJV)

Sadly, this is a picture of the Church today which has, by in large, lost its saltiness. The warning to the Church of Laodicea is that it is about to be spit out (Rev. 3:16), and the warning Jesus gives in Matthew 5:13 is: *"to be thrown out and trampled underfoot by men."*

Both of these are depictions of the Church going into the horrible Tribulation period if they do not repent in time. Now is the time to return to the Lord and to climb back up the mountain to hear Christ's words so as to be found ***"habitually hearing and habitually doing them"*** once again.

Light of the World

> *"14) You are the light of the world. A city that is set on a hill cannot be hidden. 15) Nor do they light a lamp and put it under a basket, but on a lampstand, and it gives light to all who are in the house. 16) Let your light so shine before men, that they may see your good works and glorify your Father in heaven."*
> (Matthew 5:14-16 – NKJV)

Jesus also describes His disciples as being the light of the world. Again, we need to remember that Jesus had just finished describing the qualities and characteristics of the successful overcomer. These are the ones who are also called to be the *"light of the world."* The main function of light is to shine and illuminate the darkness. The overcomers' main influence should be to light up a clear path for others to follow. The world is filled with darkness, but the overcomer knows the proper direction that has been illuminated for them by the Holy Spirit in God's word. Because the mature overcomer realizes the immense importance of Christ's message they are boldly *"letting their light shine before men so that they may see their good works and glorify their Father in heaven."*

These "good works" represent works done in the power of the Holy Spirit which God prepared in advance for us to do:

> *"For we are His workmanship, created in Christ Jesus for good works, which God prepared beforehand that we should walk in them."* (Ephesians 2:10 – NKJV)

While the faithful overcomers are busy carrying out the works God created them to perform, many modern day believers are too afraid to even discuss *"works,"* because they have been taught that they were saved by grace and they don't need to be worried about works. They are pictured by Christ as placing their lamps under a basket. May this be motivation for all to raise their lamps high – back on the lampstand for the entire world to see.

The whole purpose of performing good works is to bring glory to God. The believer who exhibits the characteristics of an overcomer will not only be leading people out of darkness, but also be lighting the way for them to inherit the Kingdom:

> *"...to open their eyes, in order to turn them from darkness to light, and from the power of Satan to God, that they may receive forgiveness of sins and an* **inheritance among those who are sanctified by faith in Me.** *"* (Acts 26:18 – NKJV)

I am the Lord thy God

Thou shalt have no other gods before me

Thou shalt not make unto thee any graven image

Thou shalt not take the name of the Lord thy God in vain

Remember the sabbath day to keep it holy

Honor thy father and thy mother

Thou shalt not kill

Thou shalt not commit adultery

Thou shalt not steal

Thou shalt not bear false witness

Thou shalt not covet

Moses climbed down Mount Sinai to give the people God's laws written in stone. Jesus said that whoever keeps and teaches these commandments shall be called great in the coming Kingdom.

Chapter 3 – Overcomers' Standards

"17) Do not think that I came to destroy the Law or the Prophets. I did not come to destroy but to fulfill. 18) For assuredly, I say to you, till heaven and earth pass away, one jot or one tittle will by no means pass from the law till all is fulfilled. 19) Whoever therefore breaks one of the least of these commandments, and teaches men so, shall be called least in the kingdom of heaven; but whoever does and teaches them, he shall be called great in the kingdom of heaven. 20) For I say to you, that unless your righteousness exceeds the righteousness of the scribes and Pharisees, you will by no means enter the kingdom of heaven." (Matthew 5:17-20 – NKJV)

Christ Fulfills the Law

As was discussed earlier, Christ did not come to get rid of the law, but to fulfill it. The law of the Old Testament was given by God to Moses for people to follow. These laws were for their own good because God loves mankind and He wants what is best for us.

In this portion of His Sermon, Jesus is warning against those who teach it is alright to break the commandments. This is rampant in today's Church where grace has become a bandage to cover an unclean life. Modern day teachers try to persuade their followers that they are saved by God's grace and they are no longer under the law. In the above passage, Jesus warns that those who teach this will be called *"least in the Kingdom..."*

Not only are we to keep the commandments of the old law, Jesus came to give us an entirely new law. The Apostle Paul refers to this new law when he said:

*"Bear ye one another's burdens, and so fulfill the **law of Christ.**"* (Galatians 6:2)

Here the Apostle Paul was referring to the New Testament law that Jesus is giving us in this Sermon on the Mount. This entire sermon represents Christ's teachings (*law of Christ*) that need to be followed for the overcomer to gain their own entrance into the coming Kingdom.

In the above portion of the Sermon Jesus is telling us that our righteousness must exceed the righteousness of even the spiritual leaders of His day. The scribes and the Pharisees were supposedly the most righteous people on earth. So how can our righteousness ever exceed theirs?

We need to remember that the Christian's righteousness is based upon the imputed righteousness of Christ that is obtained by faith:

> *"Even the righteousness of God which is by faith of Jesus Christ unto all and upon all them that believe..."*
> (Romans 3:22)

Faith in Jesus Christ is the only thing that will justify a person before God. The believer receives the righteousness of God by faith in Jesus Christ + nothing.

After a person receives the righteousness of God through faith in Jesus Christ the **overcomer** will also *"hunger and thirst after righteousness."* As a result, they will be filled with God's Spirit and thereby be able to live righteously as God requires:

> *"4) That the righteousness of the law might be fulfilled in us, who walk not after the flesh, but after the Spirit. 5) For they that are after the flesh do mind the things of the flesh; but they that are after the Spirit the things of the Spirit."* (Romans 8:4-5)

While the Christian is justified through faith in the sight of God, the **overcomer** continues **to walk after the Spirit** and not after the flesh. The overcomer earnestly seeks God's righteousness by being led by the Spirit of God and not by the flesh. Only in this way will their righteousness exceed that of the scribes and Pharisees, and thereby gain them entrance into the Kingdom.

Jesus then begins evaluating some of the laws of the Old Testament with the new standards of His laws. While the Mosaic laws relate to outward actions, the new *laws of Christ* deal with the intent of the heart.

Murder

> *"21) You have heard that it was said to those of old, 'You shall not murder, and whoever murders will be in danger of the judgment.' 22) But I say to you that whoever is **angry** with his brother without a cause shall be in danger of the judgment. And whoever says to his brother, '**Raca!**' shall be in danger of the council. But whoever says, '**You fool!**' shall be in danger of hell fire. 23) Therefore if you bring your gift to the altar, and there remember that your brother has something against you, 24) leave your gift there before the altar, and go your way. First be reconciled to your brother, and then come and offer your gift. 25) Agree with your adversary quickly, while you are on the way with him, lest your adversary deliver you to the judge, the judge hand you over to the officer, and you be thrown into prison. 26) Assuredly, I say to you, you will by no means get out of there till you have paid the last penny."* (Mat. 5:21-26)

Jesus begins by comparing the Old Testament commandment of murder with His higher requirements dealing with anger. He then lists three gradations of anger and the consequences of not dealing with it properly.

The first form of anger Jesus addresses is to be angry with a brother (i.e. fellow Christian) without a valid reason. The penalty for such an act is to be in danger at the Judgement Seat of Christ where Jesus will be the final adjudicator. He goes on to explain the urgency of being reconciled with your brother quickly (i.e. now in this age before you will be required to stand before His Judgement Seat – for more information on this coming Judgement, please see Chapter 2 of our book: *THE KINGDOM* available at: www.ProphecyCountdown.com).

The second form of anger is to call your brother "*Raca*," which means (#4469) an empty headed man, which was a term of reproach. The danger for such behavior is to be brought before the "*council*" (#4892) which was an assembly of judges and magistrates that would be convened to pass judgement. This appears to be an additional level of punishment to be meted out for such intense anger.

In the final type of anger the Christian calls his brother: "*a fool*" (#3474) with the punishment being: "*hell fire*" (#1067).

To call a fellow Christian a fool is to judge him as "a foolish and godless" individual. The only one who can judge another person is God, himself. For a Christian to do this is to put himself in God's place. Such an unwarranted judgement will be punishable by: "*Gehenna*." (This is the correct term which was mistranslated as "*hell fire*." This portion of Scripture has caused Christians a great deal of confusion because the translators miss-translated "*Gehenna*" as "*hell fire*").

The origin of this word relates to a valley outside the city of Jerusalem that was in reality a garbage dump that was constantly kept burning to destroy the filthy debris. Jesus used the term *Gehenna* to show the severe punishment that would be rendered to those **believers** who were found guilty of gross sins (not confessed and repented of as in I John 1:9 & II Peter 3:9 – Since most of the uses of the term *Gehenna*[1] are found in the Lord's Sermon on the Mount, the reader may want to see our detailed study of *Hell* and *Gehenna*, which can be found in Chapter 7 of our book: *THE KINGDOM* mentioned above).

So the Christian who calls his fellow Christian *"a fool"* will be in danger of the severe fiery judgement of *Gehenna* when they arrive before the Judgement Seat of Christ. While the Old Testament law dealt with the act of murder, the New Testament *laws of Christ* assess the varying intents of the heart. Although the Christian is not in danger of going into hell, unresolved anger can result in **severe** fiery punishment for the believer at Christ's Judgement Seat. The overcomer realizes this peril and attempts to be reconciled and at peace with those around him.

Adultery

> *"27) You have heard that it was said to those of old, 'You shall not commit adultery.' 28) But I say to you that whoever **looks at a woman to lust for her** has already **committed adultery** with her in his heart. 29) If your right eye causes you to sin, pluck it out and cast it from you; for it is more profitable for you that one of your members perish, than for your whole body to be cast into hell. 30) And if your right hand causes you to sin, cut it off and cast it from you; for it is more profitable for you that one of your members perish, than for your whole body to be cast into hell. 31) Furthermore it has been said, 'Whoever divorces his wife, let him give her a certificate of divorce.' 32) But I say to you that whoever **divorces his wife** for any reason except sexual immorality causes her to commit adultery; and whoever marries a woman who is divorced **commits adultery.***"*
> (Matthew 5:27-32 – NKJV)

While the Old Testament commandment states one should not commit adultery, Jesus takes the standard set for the overcomer to a higher level. He states that if a believer even looks at a woman to lust for her, he has already committed the act of adultery in his heart. Whereas the commandment is only concerned with the actual act of adultery, Jesus says that the overcomer must not even let their eyes look at a woman to lust for her in their own heart. While the law says the actual act is a sin, Jesus says that the sin begins in a person's heart.

James explains why even the lustful look at a woman is the real problem:

> *"14) But every man is tempted, when he is drawn away of his own lust, and enticed. 15) Then when lust hath conceived, it bringeth forth sin: and sin, when it is finished, bringeth forth death."* (James 1:14-15)

Here James shows that we can be tempted by our own evil desires and be enticed by merely looking at a woman to lust after her. This lust, if not arrested immediately, is the real sin that Jesus is warning against.

Jesus goes on to explain that the real sin of lusting after another woman is so serious that the believer should *"pluck out their right eye"* because it would be better to lose your eye than to have your whole body cast into *"hell"* (*"Gehenna"*).

These verses have been greatly misunderstood because of the mistranslation of *Gehenna* as *hell*. Christians will not be cast into hell, but if the sin of lusting after another woman in one's own heart is not held in check, the believer will be seriously punished when they appear before the Judgement Seat of Christ (**severe** fiery punishment – see I Co. 3:12-15). Does Jesus really mean a person should pluck out their eye or cut off their hand? No, these are figurative terms Jesus was employing to show the serious nature of this affront to God. He is saying that it is such a severe transgression, that the overcomer will want to take **drastic measures** to ensure that their **desires are not enticed to covet another woman in their heart**. Job, realizing the critical nature of the issue resolved in his heart:

> *"I made a **covenant with my eyes** not to **look lustfully** at a girl."* (Job 31:1 – NIV)

The Apostle Paul cautioned Titus:

> *"12) teaching us that, **denying ungodliness and worldly lusts, we should live soberly, righteously, and godly in the present age**, 13) looking for the blessed hope and glorious appearing of our great God and Savior Jesus Christ,"* (Titus 2:12-13 – NKJV)

The overcomer purposes in his heart to live a holy life with a pure heart. Whenever temptation arrives, the successful overcomer knows that it is critical to allow the Holy Spirit to be in complete control in order to crucify the old flesh nature. The overcomer knows that Jesus is coming soon (blessed hope) and is looking for Jesus every day.

While believers may sometimes give into temptation and sin, the overcomer will promptly seek forgiveness in order to restore fellowship with the Lord (I John 1:9 and II Peter 3:9).

In addition to Jesus characterizing lust as an act of adultery, he goes on to classify divorce as adultery (unless there had been sexual immorality). The Jewish leaders had allowed a divorce to be easily granted and because this was not what God originally intended for marriage, Jesus states that unwarranted divorce is the same as committing adultery.

Oaths

> *"33) Again you have heard that it was said to those of old, 'You shall not swear falsely, but shall perform your oaths to the Lord.' 34) But I say to you, do not swear at all: neither by heaven, for it is God's throne; 35) nor by the earth, for it is His footstool; nor by Jerusalem, for it is the city of the great King. 36) Nor shall you swear by your head, because you cannot make one hair white or black. 37) But **let your 'Yes,' be 'Yes' and your 'No,' 'No.'** For whatever is more than these is from the evil one."* (Matthew 5:33-37 – NKJV)

At the time of Christ, the Jews loved to make oaths and some had learned to use their oaths to be evasive. They did this by carefully wording their promises or statements without using the words, *"in the name of God"* in their promise. They would make a promise in *"the name of Jerusalem"* or *"on their own head"* and since the name of God was not in the oath, they believed they were not bound by the promise or statement.

Jesus saw through their deceit, so He introduced this new *"law of Christ"* which simply says let your *"Yes be Yes and your No be No."* By adding anything more to an oath, Jesus is saying that it comes from the deceitfulness found in the fallen nature of man – so leave it out of your oath.

Revenge

> *"38) You have heard that it was said, 'An eye for an eye and a tooth for a tooth.' 39) But I tell you not to resist an evil person. But whoever slaps you on your right cheek, turn the other to him also. 40) If anyone wants to sue you and take away your tunic, let him have your cloak also. 41) And whoever compels you to go one mile, go with him two. 42) Give to him who asks you, and from him who wants to borrow from you do not turn away."* (Matthew 5:38-42 – NKJV)

The Old Testament law found in Exodus 21:24, Leviticus 24:10, and Deuteronomy 19:21, was originally intended to limit the amount of harm that was allowed in retaliation for an injury done by another person. These punishments were intended to be carried out under the supervision of the councils, however, it had become the practice for individuals to take justice into their own hands with a type of vigilante revenge.

Jesus knew that this was a perversion of what God had intended, so He introduced these new laws for His followers to keep. All three of the examples that Christ used show that the return of evil for evil should be replaced by the return of good for evil.

In the first example, Jesus tells us we should be willing to suffer the derision of a slap on our cheek with the humility of offering our other cheek to suffer that same contempt. Or if someone sues you for your undershirt, give him your jacket as well. And if you are compelled to travel one mile (as required under Roman law at the time), cheerfully go along for an extra mile.

Jesus is showing us that the standards of the overcomer are much higher than the requirements of the old law. The overcomer is to follow in the Lord's footsteps by learning to have a meek and lowly heart that is willing to suffer wrong in humble submission. In doing these things the overcomer learns to reflect the image of Christ instead of the revenge that may have been expected.

Love Your Enemies

> *"43) You have heard that it was said, 'You shall love your neighbor and hate your enemy.' 44) But I say to you, love your enemies, bless those who curse you, do good to those who hate you, and pray for those who spitefully use you and persecute you, 45) that you may* **be sons of your Father** *in heaven; for He makes His sun rise on the evil and on the good, and sends rain on the just and on the unjust. 46) For if you love those who love you, what reward have you? Do not even the tax collectors do the same? 47) And if you greet your brethren only, what do you do more than others? Do not even the tax collectors do so? 48) Therefore you shall* **be perfect**, *just as your Father in heaven is perfect."*
> (Matthew 5:43-48 – NKJV)

Jesus concludes this section of His Sermon by teaching us how we are supposed to show love. As with all of His standards for the overcomer, Jesus raises the bar once again and tells us that we should not only love our neighbors, but also love our enemies.

We are to show this love for our enemies by blessing them, doing good to them, and praying for them. To the natural man these actions sound almost impossible, but to the person who has received the love of God in his own heart and life they become a possibility. But not all Christians are able to reach this higher standard set by our Lord. To really love our enemies requires the overcomer to allow the Spirit of God to take over. The carnal Christian will want to hold on to all of the hurt and wrong doing they have suffered by their enemy, but the overcomer will look past all of this and really seek the highest and the best for those who have wronged them.

Because the overcomer is able to really love his enemies by showing them the love of God in their lives they will be considered mature and complete sons of God reflecting the genuine nature of their Father in heaven.

The standards set by Jesus in His Sermon on the Mount are far above the previous requirements of the old law.[2] These new *"laws of Christ"* require the believer to be led by and filled with the Holy Spirit in their daily walk. Only by doing this will they become the overcomers Jesus wants them to be – reflecting God's love for everyone to see and experience.

---

*"For the commandments, "You shall not commit adultery," "You shall not murder," "You shall not steal," "You shall not bear false witness," "You shall not covet," and if there is any other commandment, **are all summed up in this saying,** namely, "You shall love your neighbor as yourself."* (Romans 13:9 – NKJV)

Chapter 4 – Overcomers' Motivation

When Jesus first sat down on the mountain, He discussed the qualities and characteristics the overcomer should exhibit along with how they should influence the world around them. He then went on to describe the new higher standards the overcomer is called to attain in order to reflect the very nature of their Father in heaven.

Jesus now turns His attention to the motivation they should exhibit in their new walk with Him by discussing three important areas of their lives: giving (good deeds), praying, and fasting.

Good Deeds

> *"1) Take heed that you do not do your charitable deeds before men, to be seen by them. Otherwise you have no reward from your Father in heaven. 2) Therefore, when you do a charitable deed, do not sound a trumpet before you as the hypocrites do in the synagogues and in the streets, that they may have glory from men. Assuredly, I say to you, they have their reward. 3) But when you do a charitable deed, do not let your left hand know what your right hand is doing, 4) that your charitable deed may be in secret; and your Father who sees in secret will Himself reward you openly."* (Matt. 6:1-4 NKJV)

Many of the Pharisees in Jesus' day loved to make their gifts openly for everyone to see. In this section of the Sermon on the Mount, Jesus is rebuking the utter hypocrisy exhibited by this behavior. While giving gifts to those in need is a wonderful thing (see Proverbs 19:17), if the motive of such generosity is to be noticed by others, then they will lose any reward from their heavenly Father. The motive for giving should be to help those in need, but if our giving is done for the praise of men we will not be rewarded for it by God which is far more valuable than the praise of man.

Giving to help those in need is a good thing and it pleases the Lord. The motive behind the gift should be one of compassion and not for recognition. The overcomer understands these principles and gives out of a pure heart of love. Anonymous gifts are an example of not letting your left hand know what your right hand is doing and will be richly rewarded by our Father in heaven.

Praying

> *"5) And when you pray, you shall not be like the hypocrites. For they love to pray standing in the synagogues and on the corners of the streets, that they may be seen by men. Assuredly, I say to you, they have their reward. 6) But you, when you pray, go into your room, and when you have shut your door, pray to your Father who is in the secret place; and your Father who sees in secret will reward you openly. 7) And when you pray, do not use vain repetitions as the heathen do. For they think that they will be heard for their many words. 8) Therefore do not be like them. **For your Father knows the things you have need of before you ask Him.**"* (Matthew 6:5-8 – NKJV)

In like manner with praying, the Lord rebukes the hypocritical practice of those whose motivation was to be noticed by other people. Many of the pious Jews loved to be seen openly praying in the streets using vain repetition or flowery words to impress upon others how holy they were. Jesus saw through this and instructs his disciple to go into their prayer closet to petition their heavenly Father. The overcomer understands these principles of prayer and is not concerned with drawing attention to themselves, but wants to draw near to God.

Fasting

> *"16) Moreover, when you fast, do not be like the hypocrites, with a sad countenance. For they disfigure their faces that they may appear to men to be fasting. Assuredly, I say to you, they have their reward. 17) But you, when you fast, anoint your head and wash your face, 18)* **so that you do not appear to men to be fasting**, *but to your Father who is in the secret place; and your Father who sees in secret will reward you openly."* (Matthew 6:16-18 – NKJV)

Finally, Jesus addresses the similar hypocrisy he witnessed by those who fasted to be noticed by men. Some of the Jews would fast in order to impress others with how spiritual they were. They would openly display their "sad countenance" to make sure others would notice they were fasting.

When the overcomer fasts they are to appear normal and not even let others know they are fasting. The entire motive for fasting should be to draw near to God in all humility as an act of contrition or self-discipline. It should be to grow in our relationship with our Father in heaven and not to impress our brothers and sisters in Christ as to how "spiritual" we are. A good practice to follow is to fast in "secret" by not letting others even know you are fasting.

Summary

While all three disciplines of giving, praying and fasting are essential Godly endeavors, if done with the wrong motive or if carried out for the wrong reasons they can become vain exhibitions designed to impress the carnal nature of man with little or no genuine spiritual value.

The phony displays carried out by the Pharisees in the days of Jesus are still carried out today in our modern society. As was mentioned in previous chapters, the lukewarm, Laodicean church of this age says:

> *"I am rich, have become wealthy, and have need of nothing'—and do not know that you are wretched, miserable, poor, blind, and naked.."* (Rev.3:17 – NKJV)

With today's great wealth, many large churches and cathedrals have been built across our land. Many times the wealthy become the leaders in these churches even though they may not be the most spiritually qualified. Their money "talks" and many pastors become reliant on the support of the wealthy instead of upon God. As a result, many of these churches don't realize that they have become spiritually poor, blind and naked because their leaders have been tainted by wrong motives. Instead of preaching biblical truth they have fulfilled Paul's prophecy:

> *"For the time will come when men will not put up with sound doctrine. Instead, to suit their own desires, they will gather around them a great number of teachers to say what their itching ears want to hear."*
> (II Timothy 4:3 – NIV)

While the overcomer will strongly object and insist on a return to sound doctrine, the security the wealthy provide will be a strong opponent. Jesus rebuked the religious leaders during His day because their entire motivation had become centered on man as opposed to focusing on pleasing God. May many of the current day leaders and teachers in the Church be convicted by our Lord's simple instruction in this portion of His Sermon and be motivated to please the Lord in all that they do.

> *"You must teach these things and encourage the believers to do them. You have the authority to correct them when necessary, so don't let anyone disregard what you say."* (Titus 2:15 – NLT)

Chapter 5 – Overcomers' Prayer

Jesus then teaches His disciples how we should pray by giving us what has come to be known as: "the Lord's Prayer."

"9) In this manner, therefore, pray:

Our Father in heaven,
Jesus tells us to pray to our Father in heaven which should give us confidence to know who we are praying to.

Hallowed be Your name.
We are to acknowledge Him with deep reverence for who He is.

*10) **Your kingdom come.***
Until Jesus returns, we are to pray for His coming Kingdom. The entire Sermon on the Mount is devoted to instructing the overcomer on how they are to live their new life as His disciple in order to qualify to enter into His coming Kingdom. Jesus lists this here as one of the top priorities they should pray for.

Your will be done On earth as it is in heaven.
Next, Jesus tells us we should submit our will on this earth to God's will in heaven. God has a perfect will (Rom. 12:2) for each of His people and He wants us to submit our life to Him.

*11) **Give us this day our daily bread.***
After recognizing God's name, God's coming Kingdom, and then God's will, Jesus then instructs us to pray for our needs in complete dependence upon Him.

Notice we are to pray only for our <u>daily</u> bread (physical food and spiritual food) for each new day. He wants us to live by faith knowing that He will supply our needs and that we do not need to worry about tomorrow's bread.

12) And forgive us our debts,
The next thing we should ask our heavenly Father for is forgiveness of any and all failings on our part. This would include our sins, trespasses and failures against Him or others.

As we forgive our debtors.
This is an acknowledgement that we are to forgive other people when they commit trespasses against us. Jesus goes into this subject later on (verses 14 and 15 below) after He completes the main points of this model prayer.

13) And do not lead us into temptation,
Jesus then tells us to pray that God will not lead us into temptation. The Greek word for temptation is # 3986 (peirasmos) which can represent a trial or test that can be sent by God and serve to test or prove one's character or faith.

It is extremely important to note that this is the exact same term that Jesus uses in His promise to the Church of Philadelphia:

> *"Since you have kept my command ("word – KJ) to endure patiently, **I will also keep you from the hour of trial** that is going to come upon the whole world to test those who live on the earth."* (Revelation 3:10 – NIV)

The Church of Philadelphia is the one faithful Church who keeps God's word and is given the wonderful promise of being kept from the *"hour of trial"* which represents the Tribulation period.

In other words, in the Lord's prayer, Jesus is telling the overcomer that they should be praying for God to deliver them from the coming Tribulation period. This is the promise given to the Church of Philadelphia and it is also the same prayer Jesus later instructs His disciples to pray when telling them about the day that is coming unexpectedly as a snare:

> *"34) But take heed to yourselves, lest your hearts be weighed down with carousing, drunkenness, and cares of this life, and **that Day come on you unexpectedly**. 35) For **it will come as a snare** on all those who dwell on the face of the whole earth. 36) **Watch therefore**, and **pray always that you may be counted worthy to escape all these things** that will come to pass, and to stand before the Son of Man.* (Luke 21: 34-36 – NKJV)

This confirms that there is an escape from the Tribulation period for those who are **praying** that they may be counted worthy to escape it. The overcomer will be regularly praying for God to count them worthy to be kept from the coming Tribulation period.

But deliver us from the evil one.
The very next part of the verse confirms that we are to pray for God to deliver us from the coming Antichrist who will be the ruler on the earth during the Tribulation period.

Most of the modern day Church has no idea that the Lord's prayer instructs us to pray for deliverance from the coming Tribulation period. This is one of the reasons that this chapter was called the *"Overcomers' Prayer."* The overcomer has ears to hear these instructions given to them by the Lord and they are actively praying this prayer for deliverance from the coming Tribulation period on a regular basis.

For Yours is the kingdom and the power and the glory forever. Amen.
Jesus then ends this model prayer by affirming that the Kingdom, Power and Glory all belong to God both now and forever more.

Jesus then footnotes His prayer by reminding us:
14) For if you forgive men their trespasses, your heavenly Father will also forgive you.

15) But if you do not forgive men their trespasses, neither will your Father forgive your trespasses."
(Matthew 6:9-15 – NKJV)

These concluding remarks by Jesus make it clear that it is important for us to forgive others when they commit trespasses against us. This is an important warning that the overcomer will take very seriously to ensure that they do not hold or nurse any grudges when wronged by others.

Partial or Phased Rapture[3]

It is important to point out that our Lord alludes to the doctrine of a "partial" or "phased" Rapture of believers in both the earlier and later portions of His ministry. First, in the Sermon on the Mount, Jesus teaches His disciples to pray for deliverance from the Tribulation period (v.13). Towards the very end of His ministry when He gives His famous discourse on the Mount of Olives He also instructs His followers to always pray for escape from the same Tribulation period (Luke 21:34-36 above).

Jesus chose to teach His disciples this principle of a "partial" or "phased" Rapture on two different occasions. Both times were on a "Mount," both times He taught this privately to His disciples, and both times He included this important instruction in a prayer for His disciples to follow. The overcomer has the ears to hear and the heart to understand this teaching while the rest of the Church prefers to follow the Traditions of man (Colossians 2:8).

The overcomer heeds the Lord's advice and prays for deliverance from the coming Tribulation period on a continual basis.

Chapter 6 – Overcomers' True Riches

We come into this world with nothing, and when our days on this planet come to an end, we can't take anything with us when we leave.

> *"For we brought nothing into this world, and it is certain we can carry nothing out."* (I Timothy 6:7)

Paul's instructions to Timothy serve as a backdrop for what the Lord teaches us concerning the true riches in this life.

> *"19) Do not lay up for yourselves treasures on earth, where moth and rust destroy and where thieves break in and steal; 20) but lay up for yourselves treasures in heaven, where neither moth nor rust destroys and where thieves do not break in and steal. 21) For where your treasure is, there your heart will be also."*
> (Matthew 6:19-21 – NKJV)

Jesus is telling His disciples that it is unwise to place very much value in acquiring or amassing great quantities of goods and wealth. The treasures of this earth can be easily destroyed or taken from us and the true riches in this life relate to the treasures we are laying up in heaven.

The treasures of heaven or treasures of earth relate to what the disciple is devoting his life to. Our focus can either be on the things of this earth or the things of heaven. What we focus our life on is what really matters. Jesus is advising His disciples to be focusing their life on the treasures of heaven. The overcomer is listening to the Lord's advice and truly seeking the righteousness of God with his whole heart. The treasures of heaven are God's Kingdom and God's righteousness. The overcomers' heart is devoted to seeking after these.

The overcomers' true riches come from focusing his entire life on the Lord. His allegiance is to God and His Kingdom as the top priority. Knowing that earthly riches are fleeting and temporary, the overcomers' great passion is to seek after the coming Kingdom and to help lead others down the same path.

The carnal Christian on the other hand is too concerned with the treasures of earth to care about heavenly treasures. Wealth and material possessions are their main focus which can be observed in what Christ shared next:

> *"22) The lamp of the body is the eye. If therefore your eye is good, your whole body will be full of light. 23) But if your eye is bad, your whole body will be full of darkness. If therefore the light that is in you is darkness, how great is that darkness! 24) No one can serve two masters; for either he will hate the one and love the other, or else he will be loyal to the one and despise the other. You cannot serve God and mammon."*
> (Matthew 6:22-24 – NKJV)

The eye Jesus is speaking about in the above passage relates to the spiritual eye or their spiritual perception. The overcomers' eye is *"good"* which in the Greek means: single, sound, unspotted, pure or good #573 (haplous). Their eye is set on a single purpose which is heaven whereas the bad eye lacks spiritual perception and is focused on <u>both</u> the earth and heaven. The carnal believer has poor spiritual eyesight and tries to seek after "mammon" which means earthly riches <u>and</u> heaven. As Jesus indicates, you cannot serve two different masters.

Several years ago we heard a story that helps illustrate this important teaching:

"I am reminded of a builder who once worked for a contractor. He had labored many years as a builder, erecting homes, office buildings, schools, and so on. As the years went by, this man

felt that he wasn't receiving his fair share of the wages paid out. One day the contractor gave this builder the plans for a house and told him to build it. The builder decided that this was his opportunity to gain something for himself. He planned to put into this house the cheapest of all materials, and pocket the difference between the best and least valuable goods. So the concrete was not mixed right, the wood was the cheapest kind, and the plaster was not prepared according to specifications. In every way the builder shortchanged the materials and labor that went into that house. When the house was completed the contractor said to the builder, "You know, you have worked for me these many years. It was hard for me to pay you all you were worth, but I have tried to be fair. So, in token for all you have done for me, I am giving you this house. This house is my gift to you." Suddenly the builder realized that he had built a house for himself that would quickly fall apart."

This story helps to illustrate how the carnal Christian's focus is divided. Instead of the builder constructing the best house he was capable of building to please the contractor, he decided that he had not received enough in wages – so he came up with a scheme to *"lay up treasures"* for himself. When his work was completed, he was duly rewarded for his divided loyalty.

In a similar matter, the carnal believer tries to serve the Lord, but his heart is really more concerned with his own wealth and the riches of this life than truly focusing on the Lord's business. The carnal believer will be in for a huge surprise at the Judgement Seat of Christ:

> *"9) Wherefore we labour, that, whether present or absent, we may be accepted of him. 10) For we must all appear before the judgment seat of Christ; that every one may **receive the things done** in his body, **according to that he hath done**, whether it be **good or bad**. 11) Knowing therefore the terror of the Lord, we persuade men..."* (II Corinthians 5:9-11)

May this warning from the Apostle Paul help motivate all of us to focus our lives on where our true riches may be found. In the final section of Matthew 6, Jesus introduces one of the main keys to finding these true riches.

Don't Worry

> "25) Therefore I say to you, do not worry about your life, what you will eat or what you will drink; nor about your body, what you will put on. Is not life more than food and the body more than clothing? 26) Look at the birds of the air, for they neither sow nor reap nor gather into barns; yet your heavenly Father feeds them. Are you not of more value than they? 27) Which of you by worrying can add one cubit to his stature? 28) So why do you worry about clothing? Consider the lilies of the field, how they grow: they neither toil nor spin; 29) and yet I say to you that even Solomon in all his glory was not arrayed like one of these. 30) Now if God so clothes the grass of the field, which today is, and tomorrow is thrown into the oven, will He not much more clothe you, O you of little faith? 31) Therefore do not worry, saying, 'What shall we eat?' or 'What shall we drink?' or 'What shall we wear?' 32) For after all these things the Gentiles seek. For your heavenly Father knows that you need all these things. **33) But seek first the kingdom of God and His righteousness, and all these things shall be added to you.** 34) Therefore do not worry about tomorrow, for tomorrow will worry about its own things. Sufficient for the day is its own trouble."
> (Matthew 6:25-34 – NKJV)

This is one of the most beautiful sections of the Sermon on the Mount. Jesus paints a magnificent picture for His disciples by calling their attention to the birds in the air and the picturesque lilies of the fields in the valleys below. The illustration of how our heavenly Father so lovingly cares for the birds and the flowers gives His disciples great comfort in knowing that God can also provide for all their basic necessities.

But here Jesus introduces the one great stipulation that many believers do not observe. He states that their heavenly Father already knows the things that they need. He then assures them of God's provision with this conditional promise:

> *"But **seek first the kingdom of God and His righteousness**, and all these things shall be added to you."* (Matthew 6:33 – NKJV)

Here the Lord gives us such simple instructions for real security. He says that if we really seek the Kingdom of God and His righteousness as our first priority, then all of life's basic necessities will be provided.

The key to not having to worry about having provisions is to really seek the coming Kingdom and the righteousness of God as our top priority. Jesus says that if we do this, then we will never need to worry about our temporal needs. If we seek the true riches in God's Kingdom, then He will supply us with what we need to sustain our lives in the same way He is able to provide for the birds of the air and the lilies of the field.

Oh, what a glorious promise Jesus is making to the overcomer who has the ears to listen and the heart to understand. The overcomer realizes that Christ's words are trustworthy and they resolve in their hearts to truly seek after the Kingdom of God as their primary goal. The central focus of their life becomes seeking God's righteousness and sharing this wonderful news with others.

For the overcomer, the true riches in life are found by seeking (with a pure heart) to be filled with more and more of God's righteousness. Remembering that Jesus said those who *"hunger and thirst for righteousness will be filled,"* the overcomer realizes this requires daily effort to ensure their life is truly sanctified. The Apostle Paul cautioned the Philippians:

> *"Therefore, my beloved, as you have always obeyed, so now, not only as in my presence but much more in my absence, **work out your own salvation with fear and trembling,**"* (Philippians 2:12 – ESV)

While the believer receives the imputed righteousness of Christ when they are saved, the overcomer understands the Lord is teaching them that seeking after God's Kingdom and His righteousness (Mat. 5:6) requires the daily seeking of more of His righteousness in order to sanctify their own soul.

James realizes this righteousness is received from God's word:

> *"Therefore put away all filthiness and rampant wickedness and receive with meekness **the implanted word**, which is able to save your souls."*
> (James 1:21 – ESV)

And Peter instructed us that the whole goal of our faith is the complete sanctification of our souls:

> *"Receiving the end of your faith, even the salvation of your souls."* (I Peter 1:9)

The overcomer has learned to totally yield their life to Christ and is passionate about seeking the coming Kingdom. They are not worried about earthly treasures for they know that the true riches in life are only found in God's righteousness which they deeply strive and long for every single day.

> *"For what is a man profited, if he shall gain the whole world, and lose his own soul?"*(Matthew 16:26)

Chapter 7 – Overcomers' Dealings With Others

Jesus begins the final portion in His great Sermon by giving His disciples some valuable lessons about dealing with others.

> *"1) Judge not, that you be not judged. 2) For with what judgment you judge, you will be judged; and with the measure you use, it will be measured back to you. 3) And why do you look at the speck in your brother's eye, but do not consider the plank in your own eye? 4) Or how can you say to your brother, 'Let me remove the speck from your eye'; and look, a plank is in your own eye? 5) Hypocrite! First remove the plank from your own eye, and then you will see clearly to remove the speck from your brother's eye. 6) Do not give what is holy to the dogs; nor cast your pearls before swine, lest they trample them under their feet, and turn and tear you in pieces."* (Matthew 7:1-6 – NKJV)

Do Not Judge

Jesus had already made it clear in His model prayer (Chapter 5) that it is important for us to forgive others when they commit trespasses against us and to ensure that we do not hold or nurse any grudges when we are wronged by others. Indirectly related to forgiveness is the inclination we may have to judge one another.

As holding grudges and not forgiving others will boomerang back on us, so too will our inappropriate judgement of another person. James explains why we should not judge:

> *"11) Don't speak evil against each other, dear brothers and sisters. If you criticize and judge each other, then you are criticizing and judging God's law. But your job is to obey the law, not to judge whether it applies to you.*

12) God alone, who gave the law, is the Judge. He alone has the power to save or to destroy. So what right do you have to judge your neighbor?"
(James 4:11-12 – NLT)

Jesus knew that the natural tendency of man is to be critical of others. Jesus warns His disciples to not judge others because God will use the same evaluation methods on us that we use on others. Since God alone has the right and the power to judge others, the overcomer realizes that it is not his place to judge anyone else.

At this point, Jesus interjects His sense of humor in the illustration and uses it to show how ludicrous our judgement of others can be. One can almost visualize a person with a large board covering their own eyes trying to remove a tiny little speck from another party. Jesus drives home the point how hypocritical it is for anyone to attempt to judge another person and the Lord's beautiful illustration will not easily be forgotten.

The Unteachable

Jesus continues to use vivid images to drive home a point about another matter: *"6) Do not give what is holy to the dogs; nor cast your pearls before swine, lest they trample them under their feet, and turn and tear you in pieces."*

Here Jesus is telling His disciples not to even attempt to teach the unteachable. The dogs and the swine both represent animals that were considered unholy and unclean. It was forbidden for the Jews to eat these animals. The Lord is instructing them not to give their holy and valuable advice to those who are known to be unholy and unteachable. David offered similar counsel:

"7) Whoever corrects a mocker invites insult; whoever rebukes a wicked man incurs abuse. 8) Do not rebuke a mocker or he will hate you; rebuke a wise man and he will love you." (Proverbs 9:7-8 – NIV)

The overcomer would be wise to heed this advice and not attempt to share holy truths and experiences with those who are unteachable and unable to receive such spiritual wisdom. Jesus is advising us to avoid such people for our own good.

Ask, Seek, and Knock

Jesus continues His teaching on our dealings with others by using an analogy of how our heavenly Father deals with His own children:

> *"7) **Ask**, and it will be given to you; **seek**, and you will find; **knock**, and it will be opened to you.   8) For everyone who asks receives, and he who seeks finds, and to him who knocks it will be opened.   9) Or what man is there among you who, if his son asks for bread will give him a stone?   10) Or if he asks for a fish, will he give him a serpent?   11) If you then, being evil, know how to give good gifts to your children, how much more will your Father who is in heaven give good things to those who ask Him!   12) Therefore, whatever you want men to do to you, do also to them, for this is the Law and the Prophets."* (Matthew 7:7-12 – NKJV)

By using of the terms: *ask, seek* and *knock* the Lord is giving His disciples a beautiful synopsis of some of the most significant instructions covered in His sermon.

First, Jesus tells us to *"ask"* and it will be given.   The instruction to ask refers to the overcomer asking to enter into the coming Kingdom.   The entire object of the Sermon on the Mount concerns the believer's ability to enter the Kingdom. In teaching us how to pray, our Lord made it clear that we need to continually be praying for our deliverance from the coming Tribulation period:

> *"And do not lead us into temptation, but deliver us from the evil one..."* (Matthew 6:13 – NKJV)

The reader may want to review Chapter 5, pages 46 to 47 where this important prayer for deliverance was discussed. The overcomer should be persistently asking the Lord to be counted worthy of escaping the coming Tribulation period and to be able to enter into the coming Kingdom.

Second, the Lord says we should *"seek"* and we will find. This refers to His instruction in Chapter 6:

> *"But **seek first** the kingdom of God and His righteousness, and all these things shall be added to you."* (Matthew 6:33 – NKJV)

Here Jesus is telling us that we should continually be seeking our own entrance into the coming Kingdom. The overcomer has set God's Kingdom and His righteousness as the number one priority in his life and is constantly seeking the Kingdom of God on a continual basis.

Finally, Jesus says we should *"knock"* and it will be opened for us. One *"knocks"* on either a door or a gate. The reference Jesus is making to knocking relates to the gate that He is getting ready to discuss just a few short verses later. This important gate will be discussed in the following chapter, but suffice it to say for now, our Lord wants the overcomer to continue knocking on that gate until it is opened for him.

The Lord continues His analogy of how we should deal with others by giving the example of how we would not give our children a stone if they asked for bread or hand them a snake if they asked for a fish. In the same way, our heavenly Father will surely give His children good things which they ask for.

The Golden Rule

Jesus then completes His comparison of how God deals with His children to teach His disciples how we should treat others.

> *"Therefore, whatever you want men to do to you, do also to them, for this is the Law and the Prophets."* (Matthew 7:12 – NKJV)

In the same manner that God knows how to give good things to His children, the overcomer is to treat others as they would want to be treated by them.

If we ask God for bread, He is not going to give us a stone. In like manner, if our neighbor asked us for a loaf of bread we certainly would not give them a stone. And if we asked them for a fish, we surely would not be expecting a snake.

The "golden rule" simply means we should treat other people in the same way we would want them to treat us. Also, remember it was previously discussed how Jesus said the whole Law and the Prophets are summed up:

> *"36) 'Teacher, which is the great commandment in the law?' 37) Jesus said to him, 'You shall love the LORD your God with all your heart, with all your soul, and with all your mind.' 38) 'This is the first and great commandment. 39) And the second is like it: 'You shall love your neighbor as yourself.' 40) On these two commandments hang all the Law and the Prophets."* (Matthew 22:36-40)

In all interactions with other people, the overcomer tries to ask the question, "How would I want to be treated in this situation?" In all relationships with others, the overcomer will attempt to treat people in the same manner that they would like to be treated themselves.

In our dealings with others, the love of God should shine forth and be exhibited in all of our conduct. This will surely be the case for the overcomer who is filled with and led by the Spirit. The fruit of the Spirit will be on constant display as the love of God is truly felt by others.

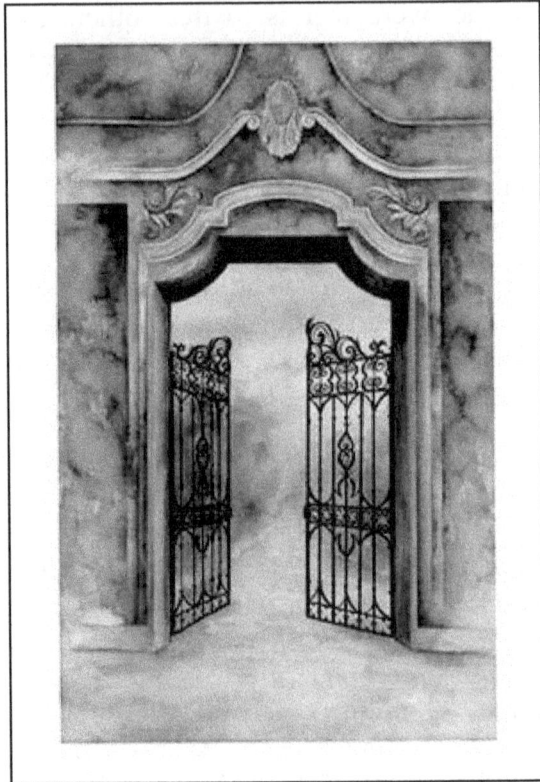

"Because narrow is the gate and difficult is the way which leads to life, and there are few who find it."
(Matthew 7:14 – NKJV)

Chapter 8 – Overcomers' Priorities

Jesus is now coming to the conclusion of His lengthy Sermon that has included some rather demanding requirements. The disciples had been challenged with nine characteristic that they should possess, as well as many new "*laws of Christ*" which went beyond the outward requirements of the law to look much deeper into the motives and intent of the heart.

By now, the disciples had realized that Jesus was teaching them about a lot more than just going to heaven. They had willingly followed Jesus up on top of the mountain and were privileged to hear remarkable instructions on how they would be allowed to enter into the coming Kingdom if they were found faithful. And they also realized that entrance into the coming Kingdom could only be obtained by persistently asking their heavenly Father, continually seeking more and more of His righteousness and repeatedly knocking on the narrow gate:

Narrow Gate

> "*13) Enter by the narrow gate; for wide is the gate and broad is the way that leads to destruction, and there are many who go in by it. 14) Because narrow is the gate and difficult is the way which leads to life, and there are few who find it.* (Matthew 7:13-14 – NKJV)

Jesus begins to summarize His sermon by stating that the road to the coming Kingdom is not a wide highway, but a narrow path that leads to a small entrance. He is indicating that very few believers will find the narrow gate because it is a difficult path to pursue. Being an overcomer is not the easy path to follow. Overcoming the world, the flesh and the devil can be very difficult to achieve and it is much easier to simply follow the broad way which leads to destruction.

Paul referred to the difficult path and encouraged the disciples to remain faithful:

> *"...encouraging them to continue in the faith, and saying that **through many tribulations we must enter the kingdom of God.**"* (Acts 14:22 – ESV)

Entering the coming Kingdom requires a difficult path of which few Christians are even aware. Most believers are blindly following the broad popular road completely unaware of where it leads.

The destruction that Jesus refers to on this broad path relates to the unsanctified life of the believer. While the carnal Christian will still go to heaven, their unsanctified life is in danger of being destroyed at the Judgement Seat of Christ. Peter referred to this destruction when he exhorted the believer to repent:

> *"The Lord is not slack concerning His promise, as some count slackness, but is longsuffering toward us, not willing that any **should perish** but that all should come to repentance."* (II Peter 3:9 – NKJV)

The Greek word for perish in the above verse is *(Apollymi)* #622, which means to destroy. Peter is addressing the disciple (*"toward us"*) and telling them they need to repent or else they are in danger of being destroyed when they stand before the Lord (works burned up at the Judgement Seat – I Co. 3:12-15).

While the carnal Christian goes to heaven and spends eternity with the Lord, their unsanctified life will cause them to be excluded from ruling and reigning with Christ in the coming Kingdom. The overcomer realizes the peril of going down the broad path and has chosen to continue asking, seeking, and knocking in order to be able to enter into the narrow gate that leads to the Kingdom.

False Prophets

> *"15) Beware of false prophets, who come to you in sheep's clothing, but inwardly they are ravenous wolves. 16)` You will know them by their fruits. Do men gather grapes from thornbushes or figs from thistles? 17) Even so, every good tree bears good fruit, but a bad tree bears bad fruit. 18) A good tree cannot bear bad fruit, nor can a bad tree bear good fruit. 19) Every tree that does not bear good fruit is cut down and thrown into the fire. 20) Therefore by their fruits you will know them."*
> (Matthew 7:15-20 – NKJV)

The above verse is the first time the word *"beware"* is found in the New Testament. Jesus is warning His disciples that many false prophets will arrive on the scene. This is referring to many of the leaders in our Churches today. He says that we can recognize them by the fruit that they bear and that a good tree will bear good fruit.

This means if the leader exhibits the "Fruit" of the Spirit as outlined in Chapter 1 of this book, it is a fairly good indication that he is not a false prophet. If this "Fruit" of the Spirit is not in evidence, then it is may be a good idea to be on guard. As we will see in the following section, many Christian leaders are following the broad path referred to earlier.

Depart From Me

> *"21) Not everyone who says to Me, 'Lord, Lord,' shall enter the kingdom of heaven, but he who does the will of My Father in heaven. 22) Many will say to Me in that day, 'Lord, Lord, have we not prophesied in Your name, cast out demons in Your name, and done many wonders in Your name?' 23) And then I will declare to them, 'I never knew you; depart from Me, you who practice lawlessness!'"* (Matthew 7:21-23 – NKJV)

The above warning by our Lord should be a wake-up call to the Church because Jesus is referring to believers in the above passage. First, notice they are calling Him, *"Lord, Lord..."*

In I Corinthians it tells us:

> *"Therefore I tell you that no one is speaking by the Spirit of God says, "Jesus be cursed" and no one can say, "Jesus is Lord," except by the Holy Spirit."*
>
> (I Corinthians 12:3 – NIV)

The above teaches that only through the Holy Spirit can a person call Jesus their Lord. This is proof that the individuals Jesus was referring to were indeed Christians. They were calling Jesus Lord. But, notice what the Lord says to them:

> *"...I never knew you; depart from Me, you who practice lawlessness!"* (Matthew 7:23 – NKJV)

The word for *"knew"* (#1097) in the above verse can best be translated as: *to be intimately acquainted with.* In other words, although these Christians did many great works for Jesus, He never really knew them the way that He desired. While they knew Him as their Saviour, they had not really gotten acquainted with Him in an intimate way, in order to make Him their Lord – hence Jesus tells them, *"I never knew you..."*

As a result, these Christians were turned away by the Lord and they will not enter into the Kingdom to rule and reign with Christ. This is a sober warning to the Laodicean Church that the broad path they are following will lead to their destruction if they do not repent in time and start *asking*, *seeking* and *knocking* for their own entrance into the coming Kingdom. The priorities of these believers need to be radically altered in order to begin traveling on the narrow path – following the same path the overcomers are on towards the narrow gate.

Obedience to Christ

> *"24) Therefore whoever **hears these sayings** of Mine, and **does them**, I will liken him to a **wise man** who built his house on the **rock**: 25) and the rain descended, the floods came, and the winds blew and beat on that house; and it did not fall, for it was **founded on the rock**. 26) But everyone who hears these sayings of Mine, and **does not do them**, will be like a **foolish man** who built his house on the **sand**: 27) and the rain descended, the floods came, and the winds blew and beat on that house; and **it fell**. And great was its fall. 28) And so it was, when Jesus had ended these sayings, that the people were **astonished at His teaching**, 29) for He taught them as one having authority, and not as the scribes."* (Matthew 7:24-29 – NKJV)

Jesus concludes His sermon by giving the disciples a dramatic illustration of the difference between the overcomer and the carnal believer.

The overcomer not only hears the message in this great sermon, but also obediently follows the Lord's teaching. The Apostle James echo's Christ's lesson:

> *"Do not merely listen to the word, and so deceive yourselves. **Do what it says**."* (James 1:22 – NIV)

The overcomer repeatedly listens to the word of God and is found faithful – habitually doing what it says to do. Jesus says that this type of individual's life is built upon a rock that will be able to endure the testing's and trials of life. Because the overcomer has been obedient He says their life will stand. Since the entire Sermon on the Mount is about entrance into the coming Kingdom, Jesus is saying that this wise disciple will be able to enter into God's Kingdom.

The foolish man in the above story has a completely different set of priorities. This is the type of Christian who hears the same message, but decides the requirements are too difficult to follow and that it is much easier to follow his flesh. Jesus says that this individual's life is built upon sand that will not stand and hence not be able to enter into the coming Kingdom.

It is important to notice that this concluding story is not about the salvation of the individual, but concerns their ability to enter or not enter into the coming Kingdom. This illustration is addressed to Christ's disciples who have already been saved. The main issue is one of obedience and right priorities. The wise followers base their life on reading and following God's word on a habitual basis – their works will stand. The foolish don't base their life on following God's word and their works will not stand. The entire issue concerns the person's works. The overcomers' works are built on the rock which means under the direction of the Holy Spirit and they will stand. However, works done by the foolish are carried out by their flesh and their works will completely fall.

Matthew concludes this Sermon by noting that the people were **astonished by Christ's teaching** because He taught them with great authority unlike what they had ever heard.

Having read this short book, many readers may also be astonished by Christ's teachings. The perspective brought out in this book may not coincide with what you have been taught. Modern day teachers and preachers may tell you that the Sermon on the Mount should not concern you because we are saved by grace and you don't need to worry about entrance into the coming Kingdom. Christ's warning in His day may be just as appropriate for today:

> *"Woe to you, teachers of the law and Pharisees, you hypocrites! You shut the kingdom of heaven in men's faces. You yourselves do not enter, nor will you let those enter who are trying to."* (Matthew 23:13 – NIV)

Epilogue

Jesus left the multitudes and climbed up this mountain to deliver a Sermon meant to radically change the disciple's lives.

This Sermon is not one we should read through and then forget about it. Jesus gives us many challenging new teachings to follow and we should make it a practice to be habitually hearing and habitually doing them:

> *"Therefore everyone who is of such character as to be **habitually hearing** these words of mine and **habitually doing them**, shall be likened to an intelligent man who is of such a nature that he built his house upon the rocky cliff."* (Mat. 7:25 – Wuest New Testament)

When I began this manuscript the Lord showed me that I needed this as much as anyone else. The process of being a true overcomer is not easy. The world, our flesh, and the devil will attempt to defeat us every single day. In order to be successful overcomers we must continually die to self and allow the Holy Spirit to direct and empower our lives. This requires a daily victory that leads us on a narrow path that few want to follow.

Writing this book has inspired this author with the desire to climb back up the Mountain on a repeated basis. We need to be continually hearing our Lord's instructions on how to be the overcomer He wants us to be and allow Him to guide us on the narrow path that will lead us to His coming Kingdom. Realizing that none of the requirements laid out in this Sermon can be met in our own strength, the overcomer learns to place his life in Christ's hands:

> *"I am the vine, you are the branches. He who abides in Me, and I in him, bears much fruit; for without Me you can do nothing."* (John 15:5 – NKJV)

Only by abiding in Jesus and being filled with the Holy Spirit can we exhibit the fruit of His life to this fallen world.

May the reader be encouraged to join in the climb up this Mountain on a regular basis and to seek His Kingdom until the Lord returns. May the Lord help you be the overcomer Jesus wants you to be.

> *"28) Come to Me, all you who labor and are heavy laden, and I will give you rest. 29) Take My yoke upon you and learn from Me, for I am gentle and lowly in heart, and you will find rest for your souls. 30) For My yoke is easy and My burden is light."*
> (Matthew 11:28-30 – NKJV)

Reference Notes

Chapter 3

1) The following Scriptures mistranslated the word **Gehenna** as hell (Jesus would have used the word **Hades** if He meant hell):

*"But I say unto you, That whosoever is angry with his brother without a cause shall be in danger of the judgement: and whosoever shall say to his brother, Raca, shall be in danger of the council: but whosoever shall say, Thou fool, shall be in danger of **hell fire** (Gehenna)."* (Matthew 5:22)

*"And if thy right eye offend thee, pluck it out, and cast it from thee: for it is profitable for thee that one of thy members should perish, and not that thy whole body should be cast into **hell** (Gehenna)."* (Matthew 5:29)

*"And if thy right hand offend thee, cut it off, and cast it from thee: for it is profitable for thee that one of thy members should perish, and not [that] thy whole body should be cast into **hell** (Gehenna)."* (Matthew 5:30)

*"And if thine eye offend thee, pluck it out, and cast it from thee: it is better for thee to enter into life with one eye, rather than having two eyes to be cast into **hell fire** (Gehenna)."* (Matthew 18:9)

*"And if thy hand offend thee, cut it off: it is better for thee to enter into life maimed, than having two hands to go into **hell** (Gehenna), into the fire that never shall be quenched..."* (Mark 9:43)

*"And if thy foot offend thee, cut it off: it is better for thee to enter halt into life, than having two feet to be cast into **hell** (Gehenna), into the fire that never shall be quenched..."* (Mark 9:45)

*"And if thine eye offend thee, pluck it out: it is better for thee to enter into the kingdom of God with one eye, than having two eyes to be cast into **hell fire**..."* *(Gehenna)* (Mark 9:47)

*"And fear not them which kill the body, but are not able to kill the soul: but rather fear him which is able to destroy both soul and body in **hell** (Gehenna)."* (Matthew 10:28)

*"But I will forewarn you whom ye shall fear: Fear him, which after he hath killed hath power to cast into **hell** (Gehenna); yea, I say unto you, Fear him."* (Luke 12:5)

*"And the tongue is a fire, a world of iniquity: so is the tongue among our members, that it defileth the whole body, and setteth on fire the course of nature; and it is set on fire of **hell** (Gehenna)."* (James 3:6)

In the above verses, Jesus used the word **Gehenna** instead of Hades. While **Gehenna** has been mistranslated as hell, it does represent a severe judgement by fire for unfaithful, carnal believers. Please see Chapter 7 of **THE KINGDOM** for a detailed study of this subject: www.ProphecyCountdown.com

2) Robert Govett says in his book **Kingdom of God Future**:

> "...in the Sermon on the Mount...He was teaching those who would listen, the principles which were to guide their conduct, **if they would enter the millennial Kingdom....New principles of far greater height and depth** than the old ones of the Law are in the Sermon on the Mount disclosed by Jesus. They were God's words put into His mouth. While they were "sayings of mine," as He says; they were still "the will of His Father in heaven."

Robert Govett, **Kingdom of God Future**, 1985, page 102, Conley & Schoettle Publishing Co., (Originally 1870)
Also, please see: www.schoettlepublishing.com

Chapter 5

3) For an interesting study on the "partial" or "phased" Rapture, please see: *"Oil in Your Vessel"* by A. B. Simpson (founder of the Christian Missionary Alliance). This article can be found on our website: www.ProphecyCountdown.com (Kingdom Tab)

Also, for an excellent study of the Sermon on the Mount, please see Lyn Mize's website:

www.ffruits.org/firstfruits02/sermononthemount.html

As outlined in this book, in the Sermon on the Mount Jesus was teaching Christians on the principles needed to enter into the coming Kingdom. All disciples of Jesus Christ would do well to spend time reading and studying this great verse-by-verse exegesis by Lyn which lays out the principles that Christians should follow in order to enter into the Kingdom.

Other Recommended Books and Websites:

The following books and websites are highly recommended for those Christians who want to learn more about the deeper Truths found in the Scripture relating to ruling and reigning in the coming King's dominion:

The Open Door
by Lyn Mize   www.ffruits.org
The Gospel of the Kingdom
by Pastor Randy Shupe   www.pastorrandyshupe.com
Judgment Seat of Christ
by D.M. Panton   www.schoettlepublishing.com
Reflections of His Image
by Nancy Missler   www.kingshighway.org
The Gospel of the Kingdom
by T. Austin-Sparks   www.austin-sparks.net
Wonders of the Universe (Astronomy Picture Of the Day)   http://apod.nasa.gov/apod/astropix.html

ARE YOU READY TO
RULE AND REIGN WITH CHRIST?

"The Spirit and the Bride say, Come..."
(Revelation 22:17)

"I the LORD search the heart and test the mind, to give every man according to his ways, according to the fruit of his deeds." (Jeremiah 17:10 – ESV)

"Because narrow is the gate and difficult is the way which leads to life, and there are few who find it."
(Matthew 7:14 – NKJV)

Appendix A – Overcomers' Rewards

It is essential for all Christians to comprehend what the following Scriptures are promising to those who are overcomers. The God of the Universe is offering astonishing and fantastic rewards for successfully overcoming the world, the flesh and the devil.

> *"He that hath an ear, let him hear what the Spirit saith unto the churches; To him that **overcometh** will I give to **eat of the tree of life,** which is in the midst of the paradise of God.* (Rev. 2:7)

> *"He that hath an ear, let him hear what the Spirit saith unto the churches; To him that **overcometh** will I give to **eat of** the **hidden manna,** and will give him a **white stone,** and in the stone a **new name** written, which no man knoweth saving he that receiveth it."* (Rev. 2:17)

> *"And he that **overcometh,** and keepeth my works unto the end, to him will I give **power over the nations"*** (Rev. 2:26)

> *"Him that **overcometh** will I make a **pillar in the temple** of my God, and he shall go no more out: and I will write upon him the **name of my God,** and the **name of the city** of my God, which is new Jerusalem, which cometh down out of heaven from my God: and I will write upon him **my new name.*** (Rev. 3:12)

> *"To him that **overcometh** will I grant to **sit with me in my throne,** even as I also overcame, and am set down with my Father in his throne.* (Rev. 3:21)

> *"He that **overcometh** shall **inherit all things;** and I will be his God, and he shall be my son."* (Rev. 21:7)

Excerpt from THE COMING SPIRITUAL EARTHQUAKE

An overcomer is a believer who has had an authentic experience with God. Though thrown into the furnace of affliction, they have come forth as pure gold. The overcomer is born through the victory they receive by trusting in Jesus Christ. Learning to be an overcomer is perhaps the most difficult thing to do on this earth as a human being. Possessing impressive credentials and degrees offer little solace when it comes to where the "rubber meets the road." Every professing Christian must learn to be an overcomer through faith and total trust in their Savior. In Matthew 11:28-30, Jesus urges: *"Come unto me, all ye that labour and are heavy laden, and I will give you rest. Take my yoke upon you, and learn of me; for I am meek and lowly in heart: and ye shall find rest unto your souls. For my yoke is easy, and my burden is light."* The overcomers take their agony and burdens to the mighty counselor. Through prayer and trust, Jesus leads the downcast believer to "green pasture." The sting of the adversary is somehow turned to sweet victory. Christ alone is able to provide the peace that passes all understanding. While every believer will have trials and testing in this world, Christ reminded us to be of good cheer because He overcame this world. As believers, we find our sweet victory in Him! Overcomers are believers who find their strength and help in Him--not through man, but by the power of the Son of God. A genuine overcomer follows in Christ's footsteps. They learn to "take it on the chin" and to "take it to the cross." Whatever the world dishes out is handled with prayer and placed on the altar before God. By offering everything to Christ, they find hope and sufficiency in Him. Being an overcomer is what being a Christian is all about. Through the trials of this life, the overcomers' faith is put on trial and thereby confirmed as Holy evidence before a mighty God, it is authentic. As our example, Jesus endured the cross for the joy set before Him. Overcomers have the victory because of His victory. Through His victory, the overcomer is able to walk in newness of life. The overcomer knows: they have been crucified with Christ and their old life is gone (Gal.2:20). By dying to self, the overcomer experiences the joy of Christ's triumph in their life. Finally, an overcomer is grateful and humble: for they know of God's rich mercy and marvelous grace. If it wasn't for Christ, they would be doomed. Out of this gratitude, rises the song of gladness and praise. An overcomers' heart bursts forth with praise and adoration unto their God for the victory He provides. The overcomer knows, first hand, that while weeping may endure for the night: joy cometh in the morning!

Appendix B – Sermon on the Mount

Matthew – Chapter 5

"1) And seeing the multitudes, He went up on a mountain, and when He was seated His disciples came to Him. 2) Then He opened His mouth and taught them, saying: 3) Blessed are the poor in spirit, For theirs is the kingdom of heaven. 4) Blessed are those who mourn, For they shall be comforted. 5) Blessed are the meek, For they shall inherit the earth. 6) Blessed are those who hunger and thirst for righteousness, For they shall be filled. 7) Blessed are the merciful, For they shall obtain mercy. 8) Blessed are the pure in heart, For they shall see God. 9) Blessed are the peacemakers, For they shall be called sons of God. 10) Blessed are those who are persecuted for righteousness' sake, For theirs is the kingdom of heaven. 11) Blessed are you when they revile and persecute you, and say all kinds of evil against you falsely for My sake. 12) Rejoice and be exceedingly glad, for great is your reward in heaven, for so they persecuted the prophets who were before you. 13) You are the salt of the earth; but if the salt loses its flavor, how shall it be seasoned? It is then good for nothing but to be thrown out and trampled underfoot by men. 14) You are the light of the world. A city that is set on a hill cannot be hidden. 15) Nor do they light a lamp and put it under a basket, but on a lampstand, and it gives light to all who are in the house. 16) Let your light so shine before men, that they may see your good works and glorify your Father in heaven. 17) Do not think that I came to destroy the Law or the Prophets. I did not come to destroy but to fulfill. 18) For assuredly, I say to you, till heaven and earth pass away, one jot or one tittle will by no means pass from the law till all is fulfilled. 19) Whoever therefore breaks one of the least of these commandments, and teaches men so, shall be called least in the kingdom of heaven; but whoever does and teaches them, he shall be called great in the kingdom of heaven. 20) For I say to you, that unless your righteousness exceeds the righteousness of the scribes and Pharisees, you will by no

means enter the kingdom of heaven. 21) You have heard that it was said to those of old, 'You shall not murder, and whoever murders will be in danger of the judgment.' 22) But I say to you that whoever is angry with his brother without a cause shall be in danger of the judgment. And whoever says to his brother, 'Raca!' shall be in danger of the council. But whoever says, 'You fool!' shall be in danger of hell fire. 23) Therefore if you bring your gift to the altar, and there remember that your brother has something against you, 24) leave your gift there before the altar, and go your way. First be reconciled to your brother, and then come and offer your gift. 25) Agree with your adversary quickly, while you are on the way with him, lest your adversary deliver you to the judge, the judge hand you over to the officer, and you be thrown into prison. 26) Assuredly, I say to you, you will by no means get out of there till you have paid the last penny. 27) You have heard that it was said to those of old, 'You shall not commit adultery.' 28) But I say to you that whoever looks at a woman to lust for her has already committed adultery with her in his heart. 29) If your right eye causes you to sin, pluck it out and cast it from you; for it is more profitable for you that one of your members perish, than for your whole body to be cast into hell. 30) And if your right hand causes you to sin, cut it off and cast it from you; for it is more profitable for you that one of your members perish, than for your whole body to be cast into hell. 31) Furthermore it has been said, 'Whoever divorces his wife, let him give her a certificate of divorce.' 32) But I say to you that whoever divorces his wife for any reason except sexual immorality causes her to commit adultery; and whoever marries a woman who is divorced commits adultery. 33) Again you have heard that it was said to those of old, 'You shall not swear falsely, but shall perform your oaths to the Lord.' 34) But I say to you, do not swear at all: neither by heaven, for it is God's throne; 35) nor by the earth, for it is His footstool; nor by Jerusalem, for it is the city of the great King. 36) Nor shall you swear by your head, because you cannot make one hair white or black. 37) But let your 'Yes,' be 'Yes' and your 'No,' 'No.' For whatever is more than these is from the evil one. 38) You have heard that it was said, 'An eye for an eye and a tooth for a tooth.' 39) But I tell you not to resist an evil person. But whoever slaps you on your right cheek, turn the other to him also. 40) If anyone wants to sue you and take away your tunic, let him have your cloak also. 41) And whoever compels you to go one mile, go with him two. 42) Give to him who asks you, and from him who wants to borrow from you do not turn away. 43) You have heard that it was said, 'You shall love your neighbor and hate your enemy.' 44) But I say to you, love your enemies, bless those who curse you, do good to those who hate you, and pray for those who spitefully use you and persecute you, 45) that you may be sons of your Father in heaven; for He makes His sun rise on the evil and on the good, and sends rain on the just and on the unjust. 46) For if you love those who love you, what reward have you? Do not even the tax collectors do the same? 47) And if you greet your brethren only, what do you do more than others? Do not even the tax collectors do so? 48) Therefore you shall be perfect, just as your Father in heaven is perfect.

Matthew – Chapter 6

1) Take heed that you do not do your charitable deeds before men, to be seen by them. Otherwise you have no reward from your Father in heaven. 2) Therefore, when you do a charitable deed, do not sound a trumpet before you as the hypocrites do in the synagogues and in the streets, that they may have glory from men. Assuredly, I say to you, they have their reward. 3) But when you do a charitable deed, do not let your left hand know what your right hand is doing, 4) that your charitable deed may be in secret; and your Father who sees in secret will Himself reward you openly. 5) And when you pray, you shall not be like the hypocrites. For they love to pray standing in the synagogues and on the corners of the streets, that they may be seen by men. Assuredly, I say to you, they have their reward. 6) But you, when you pray, go into your room, and when you have

*shut your door, pray to your Father who is in the secret place;
and your Father who sees in secret will reward you openly. 7)
And when you pray, do not use vain repetitions as the heathen
do. For they think that they will be heard for their many words.
8) Therefore do not be like them. For your Father knows the
things you have need of before you ask Him. 9) In this manner,
therefore, pray: Our Father in heaven, Hallowed be Your name.
10) Your kingdom come. Your will be done On earth as it is in
heaven. 11) Give us this day our daily bread. 12) And forgive
us our debts, As we forgive our debtors. 13) And do not lead us
into temptation, But deliver us from the evil one. For Yours is
the kingdom and the power and the glory forever. Amen. 14)
For if you forgive men their trespasses, your heavenly Father
will also forgive you. 15) But if you do not forgive men their
trespasses, neither will your Father forgive your trespasses.
16) Moreover, when you fast, do not be like the hypocrites, with
a sad countenance. For they disfigure their faces that they may
appear to men to be fasting. Assuredly, I say to you, they have
their reward. 17) But you, when you fast, anoint your head and
wash your face, 18) so that you do not appear to men to be
fasting, but to your Father who is in the secret place; and your
Father who sees in secret will reward you openly. 19) Do not
lay up for yourselves treasures on earth, where moth and rust
destroy and where thieves break in and steal; 20) but lay up for
yourselves treasures in heaven, where neither moth nor rust
destroys and where thieves do not break in and steal. 21) For
where your treasure is, there your heart will be also. 22) The
lamp of the body is the eye. If therefore your eye is good, your
whole body will be full of light. 23) But if your eye is bad, your
whole body will be full of darkness. If therefore the light that is
in you is darkness, how great is that darkness! 24) No one can
serve two masters; for either he will hate the one and love the
other, or else he will be loyal to the one and despise the other.
You cannot serve God and mammon. 25) Therefore I say to
you, do not worry about your life, what you will eat or what you
will drink; nor about your body, what you will put on. Is not*

life more than food and the body more than clothing? 26) Look at the birds of the air, for they neither sow nor reap nor gather into barns; yet your heavenly Father feeds them. Are you not of more value than they? 27) Which of you by worrying can add one cubit to his stature? 28) So why do you worry about clothing? Consider the lilies of the field, how they grow: they neither toil nor spin; 29) and yet I say to you that even Solomon in all his glory was not arrayed like one of these. 30) Now if God so clothes the grass of the field, which today is, and tomorrow is thrown into the oven, will He not much more clothe you, O you of little faith? 31) Therefore do not worry, saying, 'What shall we eat?' or 'What shall we drink?' or 'What shall we wear?' 32) For after all these things the Gentiles seek. For your heavenly Father knows that you need all these things. 33) But seek first the kingdom of God and His righteousness, and all these things shall be added to you. 34) Therefore do not worry about tomorrow, for tomorrow will worry about its own things. Sufficient for the day is its own trouble.

Matthew – Chapter 7

1) Judge not, that you be not judged. 2) For with what judgment you judge, you will be judged; and with the measure you use, it will be measured back to you. 3) And why do you look at the speck in your brother's eye, but do not consider the plank in your own eye? 4) Or how can you say to your brother, 'Let me remove the speck from your eye'; and look, a plank is in your own eye? 5) Hypocrite! First remove the plank from your own eye, and then you will see clearly to remove the speck from your brother's eye. 6) Do not give what is holy to the dogs; nor cast your pearls before swine, lest they trample them under their feet, and turn and tear you in pieces. 7) Ask, and it will be given to you; seek, and you will find; knock, and it will be opened to you. 8) For everyone who asks receives, and he who seeks finds, and to him who knocks it will be opened. 9)Or what man is there among you who, if his son asks for bread will give him a stone? 10) Or if he asks for a fish, will he give him a serpent? 11) If you then, being evil, know how to give good gifts to your children, how much more will your Father who is in heaven give good things to those who ask Him! 12) Therefore, whatever you want men to do to you, do also to them, for this is the Law and the Prophets. 13) Enter by the narrow gate; for wide is the gate and broad is the way that leads to destruction, and there are many who go in by it. 14) Because narrow is the gate and difficult is the way which leads to life, and there are few who find it. 15) Beware of false prophets, who come to you in sheep's clothing, but inwardly they are ravenous wolves. 16) You will know them by their fruits. Do men gather grapes from thornbushes or figs from thistles? 17) Even so, every good tree bears good fruit, but a bad tree bears bad fruit. 18) A good tree cannot bear bad fruit, nor can a bad tree bear good fruit. 19) Every tree that does not bear good fruit is cut down and thrown into the fire. 20) Therefore by their fruits you will know them. 21) Not everyone who says to Me, 'Lord, Lord,' shall enter the kingdom of heaven, but he who does the will of My Father in heaven. 22) Many will say to Me in that day, 'Lord, Lord, have we not prophesied in Your name, cast out demons in Your name, and done many wonders in Your name?' 23) And then I will declare to them, 'I never knew you; depart from Me, you who practice lawlessness!' 24) Therefore whoever hears these sayings of Mine, and does them, I will liken him to a wise man who built his house on the rock: 25) and the rain descended, the floods came, and the winds blew and beat on that house; and it did not fall, for it was founded on the rock. 26) But everyone who hears these sayings of Mine, and does not do them, will be like a foolish man who built his house on the sand: 27) and the rain descended, the floods came, and the winds blew and beat on that house; and it fell. And great was its fall. 28) And so it was, when Jesus had ended these sayings, that the people were astonished at His teaching, 29) for He taught them as one having authority, and not as the scribes."

(Matthew 5-7 – NKJV)

Appendix C

Sign of Christ's Coming

April 8, 1997

Comet Hale-Bopp Over New York City
Credit and Copyright: J. Sivo
http://antwrp.gsfc.nasa.gov/apod/ap970408.html
"What's that point of light above the World Trade Center? It's Comet Hale-Bopp! Both faster than a speeding bullet and able to "leap" tall buildings in its single orbit, Comet Hale-Bopp is also bright enough to be seen even over the glowing lights of one of the world's premier cities. In the foreground lies the East River, while much of New York City's Lower Manhattan can be seen between the river and the comet."

"As it was in the days of Noah, so it will be at the coming of the Son of Man." (Matthew 24:37 – NIV)

-81-

These words from our wonderful Lord have several applications about the Tribulation period that is about to ensnare this world.

Seas Lifted Up

Throughout the Old Testament, the time of the coming Tribulation period is described as the time when the "seas have lifted up," and also as coming in as a "flood" (please see Jeremiah 51:42, Hosea 5:10, Daniel 11:40 and Psalm 93:3-4 for just a few examples).

This is a direct parallel to the time of Noah when the Great Flood of water came to wipe out every living creature except for righteous Noah and his family, and the pairs of animals God spared. While God said He would never flood the earth again with water, the coming Judgement will be by fire (II Peter 3:10). The book of Revelation shows that approximately three billion people will perish in the terrible time that lies ahead (see Revelation 6:8 and 9:15).

2 Witnesses

A guiding principle of God is to establish a matter based upon the witness of two or more:

> *"...a matter must be established by the testimony of two or three witnesses"* (Deuteronomy 19:15 – NIV)

In 1994, God was able to get the attention of mankind when Comet Shoemaker-Levy crashed into Jupiter on the 9th of Av (on the Jewish calendar). Interestingly, this Comet was named after the "two" witnesses who first discovered it.

In 1995, "two" more astronomers also discovered another comet. It was called Comet Hale-Bopp, and it reached its closest approach to planet Earth on March 23, 1997. It has been labeled as the most widely viewed comet in the history of mankind.

Scientists have determined that Comet Hale-Bopp's orbit brought it to our solar system 4,465 years ago (see Notes 1 and 2 below). In other words, the comet made its appearance near Earth in 1997 and also in 2468 BC. Remarkably, this comet preceded the Great Flood by 120 years! God warned Noah of this in Genesis 6:3:

> *"My Spirit shall not strive with man forever, for he is indeed flesh; yet his days shall be one hundred and twenty years."*

Days of Noah
What does all of this have to do with the Lord's return? Noah was born around 2948 BC, and Genesis 7:11, tells us that the Flood took place when Noah was 600, or in 2348 BC.

Remember, our Lord told us: ***"As it was in the days of Noah, so it will be at the coming of the Son of Man."*** (Matthew 24:37 – NIV)

In the original Greek, it is saying: ***"exactly like"*** it was, so it will be when He comes (see Strong's #5618).

During the days of Noah, Comet Hale-Bopp arrived on the scene as a harbinger of the Great Flood. Just as this same comet appeared before the Flood, could its arrival again in 1997 be a sign that God's final Judgement, also known as the time of Jacob's Trouble, is about to begin?

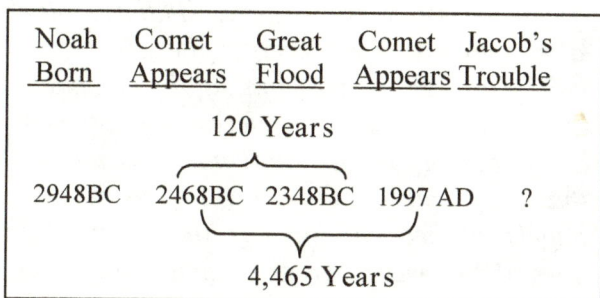

Noah Born	Comet Appears	Great Flood	Comet Appears	Jacob's Trouble
		120 Years		
2948BC	2468BC	2348BC	1997 AD	?
		4,465 Years		

Comet Hale-Bopp's arrived 120 years before the Flood as a warning to mankind. Only righteous Noah heeded God's warning and built the ark, as God instructed. By faith, Noah was obedient to God and, as a result, saved himself and his family from destruction.

Remember, Jesus told us His return would be preceded by great heavenly signs: *"And there shall be signs in the sun, and in the moon, and in the stars; and upon the earth distress of nations, with perplexity; the sea and the waves roaring..."* (Luke 21:25)

Just as this large comet appeared as a 120-year warning to Noah, its arrival in 1997 tells us that Jesus is getting ready to return again. Is this the **"Sign"** Jesus referred to?

Jesus was asked 3 questions by the disciples:
"Tell us, (1) when shall these things be" (the destruction of the city of Jerusalem), *" and (2) what shall be the __sign__ of thy coming, and (3) of the end of the world?"* (Matthew 24:3)

Sign of Christ's Coming

The **first** question had to do with events that were fulfilled in 70 AD. The **third** question has to do with the future time at the very end of the age.

The **second** question, however, has to do with the time of Christ's second coming. Jesus answered this second question in His description of the days of Noah found in Matthew 24:33-39:

> *(33)* *"So likewise ye, when ye shall see all these things, know that it is near, even at the doors. (34) Verily I say unto you, This generation shall not pass, till all these things be fulfilled. (35) Heaven and earth shall pass away, but my words shall not pass away. (36) But of that day and hour knoweth no man, no, not the angels of heaven, but my Father only. (37)* ***But as the days of Noe were, so shall also the coming of the Son***

of man be. [38]*For as in the days that were before the flood they were eating and drinking, marrying and giving in marriage, until the day that Noe entered into the ark,* [39] *And knew not until the flood came, and took them all away; so shall also the coming of the Son of man be."*

Jesus is telling us that the **sign** of His coming will be as it was during the days of Noah. As Comet Hale-Bopp was a sign to the people in Noah's day, its arrival in 1997 is a sign that Jesus is coming back again soon. Comet Hale-Bopp could be the very sign Jesus was referring to, which would announce His return for His faithful.

Remember, Jesus said, *"exactly as it was in the days of Noah, so will it be when He returns."* The appearance of Comet Hale-Bopp in 1997 is a strong indication that the Tribulation period is about to begin, but before then, Jesus is coming for His Bride!

Keep looking up! Jesus is coming again very soon!
As Noah prepared for the destruction God warned him about 120 years before the Flood, Jesus has given mankind a final warning that the Tribulation period is about to begin. The horrible destruction on 9/11 is only a precursor of what is about to take place on planet Earth. We need to be wise like Noah and prepare. Always remember our Lord's instructions:

Watch and Pray
"(34)And take heed to yourselves, lest at any time your hearts be overcharged with surfeiting, and drunkenness, and cares of this life, and so that day come upon you unawares. (35) For as a snare shall it come on all them that dwell on the face of the whole earth.(36)Watch ye therefore, and pray always, that ye may be accounted worthy to escape all these things that shall come to pass, and to stand before the Son of man" (Luke 21:34-36).

Footnotes

(1) The original orbit of Comet Hale-Bopp was calculated to be approximately 265 years by engineer George Sanctuary in his article: ***Three Craters In Israel***, published on March 31, 2001 that can be found at:

http://www.gsanctuary.com/3craters.html#3c_r13

Comet Hale-Bopp's orbit around the time of the Flood changed from 265 years to about 4,200 years. Because the plane of the comet's orbit is perpendicular to the earth's orbital plane (ecliptic), Mr. Sanctuary noted: "A negative time increment was used for this simulation…to back the comet away from the earth…. past Jupiter… and then out of the solar system. The simulation suggests that the past-past orbit had a very eccentric orbit with a period of only 265 years. When the comet passed Jupiter (***around 2203BC)*** its orbit was deflected upward, coming down near the earth 15 months later with the comet's period changed from 265 years to about (***4,200)*** years." (***added text*** *for clarity*)

(2) Don Yeomans, with NASA's Jet Propulsion Laboratory made the following observations regarding the comet's orbit: "By integrating the above orbit forward and backward in time until the comet leaves the planetary system and then referring the osculating orbital elements…the following orbital periods result: Original orbital period before entering planetary system = 4200 years. Future orbital period after exiting planetary system = 2380 years."

This analysis can be found at:

http://www2.jpl.nasa.gov/comet/ephemjpl6.html

Based upon the above two calculations we have the following:

265 [a] + 4,200 [b] = 4,465 Years

1997 AD – 4,465 Years = 2468 BC = Hale Bopp arrived

(a) Orbit period calculated by George Sanctuary before deflection around 2203 BC.

(b) Orbit period calculated by Don Yeomans after 1997 visit.

Special Invitation

This book was written to those who have been born again as mentioned in Chapter 1. If you have never been born again, would you like to be? The Bible shows that it's simple to be saved...

- Realize you are a sinner.
  "As it is written, There is none righteous, no, not one:"
                                                    (Romans 3:10)
  "... for there is no difference. For all have sinned, and come short of the glory of God;"   (Romans 3:22-23)
- Realize you CAN NOT save yourself.
  "But we are all as an unclean thing, and all our righteousness are as filthy rags; ..."   (Isaiah 64:6)
  "Not by works of righteousness which we have done, but according to his mercy he saved us, ..."   (Titus 3:5)
- Realize that Jesus Christ died on the cross to pay for your sins.
  "Who his own self bare our sins in his own body on the tree, ..."   (I Peter 2:24)
  "... Unto him that loved us, and washed us from our sins in his own blood,"   (Revelation 1:5)
- Simply by faith receive Jesus Christ as your personal Savior.
  "But as many as received him, to them gave he power to become the sons of God, even to them that believe on his name:"   (John 1:12)
  " ...Sirs, what must I do to be saved? And they said, Believe on the Lord Jesus Christ, and thou shalt be saved, and thy house."   (Acts 16:30-31)
  "...if you confess with your mouth, 'Jesus is Lord,' and believe in your heart God raised him from the dead, you will be saved."   (Romans 10:9 – NIV)

WOULD YOU LIKE TO BE SAVED?

If you want to be saved, you can receive Jesus Christ right now by making the following confession of faith:

> Lord Jesus, I know that I am a sinner, and unless you save me, I am lost forever. I thank you for dying for me at Calvary. By faith I come to you now, Lord, the best way I know how, and ask you to save me. I believe that God raised you from the dead and acknowledge you as my personal Saviour.

If you believed on the Lord, this is the most important decision of your life. You are now saved by the precious blood of Jesus Christ, which was shed for you and your sins. Now that you have received Jesus as your personal Saviour, you will want to find a Church where you can be baptized as your first act of obedience, and where the Word of God is taught so you can continue to grow in your faith. Ask the Holy Spirit to help you as you read the Bible to learn all that God has for your life.

Also, go to the Reference section of this book where you will find recommended books and websites that will help you on your wonderful journey.

Endtimes

The Bible indicates that we are living in the final days and Jesus Christ is getting ready to return very soon. This book was written to help Christians prepare for what lies ahead. The Word of God indicates that the Tribulation Period is rapidly approaching and that the Antichrist is getting ready to emerge on the world scene.

Jesus promised His disciples that there is a way to escape the horrible time of testing and persecution that will soon devastate this planet. The whole purpose of this book is to help you get prepared so you will rule and reign with Jesus when He returns.

About The Author

Jim Harman has been a Christian for more than 32 years. He has diligently studied the Word of God with a particular emphasis on Prophecy. Jim has written several books and the three most essential titles are available at www.ProphecyCountdown.com: *The Coming Spiritual Earthquake, Don't Be Left Behind, and The Kingdom;* which have been widely distributed around the world. These books encourage many to continue *"Looking"* for the Lord's soon return, and bring many to a saving knowledge of Jesus Christ.

Jim's professional experience includes being a Certified Public Accountant (CPA) and a Certified Property Manager (CPM). He has an extensive background in both public accounting and financial management with several well known national firms.

Jim has been fortunate to have been acquainted with several mature believers who understand and teach the deeper truths of the Bible. It is Jim's strong desire that many will come to realize the importance of seeking the Kingdom and seeking Christ's righteousness as we approach the soon return of our Lord and Saviour Jesus Christ.

The burden of his heart is to see many believers come to know the joy of Christ's triumph in their life as they become true overcomers; qualified and ready to rule and reign with Christ in the coming Kingdom.

To contact the author for questions or to arrange for speaking engagements:

Jim Harman
P.O. Box 941612
Maitland, FL 32794
JimHarmanCPA@aol.com

Reader's Comments

"I have read the manuscript of Jim Harman's new book **Overcomers' Guide to the Kingdom**. *I believe it is the best book that Jim has written, and it covers a topic that is vital for every Christian who wants to be found faithful at the Judgment Seat of Christ. It provides the correct interpretations of many Scriptures that are generally misunderstood by pastors and Bible teachers. It clarifies that the warnings in Scripture are for believers and not for unsaved reprobates. It also makes it clear that it is very difficult to be a faithful Christian. The book has already led me to a deeper repentance, and I will read it on a regular basis until the Lord returns."* Lyn Mize–Ooltewah, TN

"Thank you for another fine book to inspire the Believer into a closer walk with the Lord. It was a joy to read your overview of the Beatitudes in correlation with the Fruit of the Spirit. This writing presents a notable challenge to the body of Christ to come to terms with the sanctification process as you have related it. May the Lord bless both you for your hard work and the reader who takes your words to heart. May many a reader benefit from your work as they strive to accept and grow into God's will for their lives." Karen Bishop – Glasgow, Kentucky

"I always look forward and enjoy reading one of Jim Harman's books. **Overcomers' Guide to the Kingdom** *is no exception. Jim always does a beautiful job in explaining the importance of our role as overcomers in Christ. I especially love the comparisons between the Beatitudes in Matthew with "the fruit of the Spirit" in Galatians. Thanks, Jim for writing such an outstanding and necessary book in these last days."*
Robin J. Wade – Ft. Pierce, FL

"Thank you for your new book: **Overcomers' Guide to the Kingdom**. *Lots of new ideas and skillfully written."*
Nancy Missler – Coeur d'Alene, ID
The Kings Highway Ministries

Reader's Comments

"I certainly appreciate the imperative you have presented for entering into the Lord's coming Kingdom. This is a message sorely lacking at the moment. I commend your presentation of the Kingdom aspect of the Lord's message on the mountain, and that it is offering us so much more than mere salvation from sins or entrance into heaven. I also appreciate the association with the fruits of the Spirit, as this is one aspect I have not studied or considered before. Thank you my brother, I will pray for the fruit of this new book." Wayne Smith – Grove City, OH
www.LivingWalk.com

"I read Jim Harman's **Overcomers' Guide to the Kingdom** *and thought it quite good. I believe your book will greatly assist others in their journey toward the coming Kingdom as it relates the standards that will come to bear with Christians as they face our Lord at His Judgment Seat. It is indeed unfortunate that there is such little emphasis in Christendom today on personal righteousness. But then, we should not be alarmed or unsettled with the trend for what appears to surely be the last of the "last days." I support your position that personal holiness most definitely matters, particularly as it relates to the fast approaching, soon to be established, Millennial Kingdom of Jesus Christ."* Charles F. Strong – Harlingen, TX
www.Bibleone.net

"James Harman has done an amazing job in presenting a fresh and challenging look at the timeless words of Jesus found in "The Sermon on the Mount." In a day of shallow commitment and easy believism, the words of Jesus again ring true for those who would find their inheritance as genuine overcomers, "Therefore whoever hears these sayings of Mine, and does them, I will liken him to a wise man who built his house upon the rock;" Mat. 7:24 Pastor Tom Myers – Longwood, FL
Neighborhood Alliance Church

Reader's Comments

"Thank you for your new book: **Overcomers' Guide to the Kingdom**. *It is refreshing to see people awakening to the truths of accountability. These days are too dangerous, and the Devil rages with deception and temptation. It is no time to go soft, and spiritualize the Lord's warnings concerning fire, stripes, gnashing of teeth, cut asunder, etc. Jesus taught us in Matthew 13, that the interpretation of His parables are literal concerning judgments. I am sincerely thankful for your insight into these issues. I pray more would awake to see these things and make sure they understand the Lord's judgments – for in these days, it just may be that it will make the difference between a person enduring...or not. We sometimes forget that these warnings are used so we may move with fear and resist sin. When sinful temptation is raging, it just may be that some will need the full force of the Lord's warnings."*

Pastor Joey Faust – Venus, TX
Author of **The Rod-Will God Spare It?**

"This book is the "crown jewel" of all of Jim's writings. His first book **The Coming Spiritual Earthquake** *piqued my longing heart "to know and be known" of CHRIST more intimately. This teaching has found for us "the Pearl of great price and the lost Coin" of biblical teaching that's so missing today. There surely is the Coming Kingdom of our LORD to this Earth one Day very soon prepared to honor those "who have loved not their lives unto death" but have taken up their Cross and followed CHRIST. This book is written in the common man's language that even a child can understand. May all who read it be numbered among those to hear: "Well done good and faithful servant...enter into MY Joy."* Joan Olsen–Edmond, OK

Once a person is saved, the number one priority should be seeking entrance into the Kingdom through the salvation of their soul. It is pictured as a runner in a race seeking a prize represented by a crown that will last forever.

The salvation of the soul and entrance into the coming Kingdom are only achieved through much testing and the trial of one's faith. If you are going through difficulty, then REJOICE:

"Blessed is the man who perseveres under trial, because when he has stood the test, he will receive the crown of life that God has promised to those who love Him." (James 1:12)

The "Traditional" teaching on the "THE KINGDOM" has taken the Church captive into believing all Christians will rule and reign with Christ no matter if they have lived faithful and obedient lives, or if they have been slothful and disobedient with the talents God has given them. Find out the important Truth before Jesus Christ returns.

MUST READING FOR EVERY CHRISTIAN

Jesus Christ is returning for His faithful overcoming followers. Don't miss the opportunity of ruling and reigning with Christ in the coming KINGDOM!

Download your FREE copy: www.ProphecyCountdown.com

Or from Amazon.com – Available in Paperback and or Kindle Edition

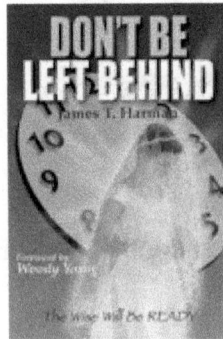

Is Daniel's Clock about to Start Ticking once again?
The recovery of the Old City of Jerusalem in June 1967 was a pivotal Prophetic Event. Find out how this major Prophetic Milestone may correlate with the start of the Second Half of Daniel's 70th Week.

> *"See to it that no one takes you captive through hollow and deceptive philosophy, which depends on human tradition and the basic principles of this world rather than on Christ."* (Colossians 2:8 NIV)

The "Traditional" teaching on the "70th Week of Daniel" has taken the Church captive into believing almost a "fairy tale" regarding Endtime events. Find out the beautiful Truth that has been hidden from modern day Christians.

MUST READING FOR EVERY CHRISTIAN

Jesus Christ is returning for His Bride. Are you "Watching" for your Bridegroom today? Find out the consequences of not being ready before the final grains of sand descend through the hour glass. Don't be one of those who will be LEFT BEHIND!

Order your copy today from www.ProphecyCountdown.com

Or from Amazon.com – Available in Paperback and or Kindle Edition

HELP DISTRIBUTE THIS MESSAGE

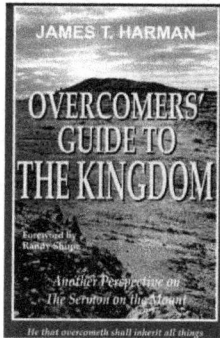

This book: *OVERCOMERS' GUIDE TO THE KINGDOM* may be reproduced and given freely to loved ones, friends, and all those who fear God. Please do not make changes to the material. Permission is required for reproduction for resale. An electronic copy (PDF) of this book is available for free at: www.ProphecyCountdown.com. Permission is granted to save the PDF copy to your computer and e-mail to all your friends.

Order Extra Paperback Copies*

# of Copies	Total Costs (Includes Shipping & Handling)
1	$ 7
5	$ 25
10	$ 45
25	$100

*Order extra copies to give to friends and loved ones.
Please send check to: Jim Harman
                       P.O. Box 941612
                       Maitland, FL 32794
Or place your order online at Amazon.com

*"The end of the age is coming soon. Therefore
be earnest, thoughtful men of prayer."*
(I Peter 4:7 – Paraphrase)

LOOKING FOR THE SON
Lyrics by Jim Harman
To Adel's hit tune: *"ROLLING IN THE DEEP"*

Lyric	Scripture
There's a fire burning in my heart	Luke 24:32
Yearning for the Lord to come,	Rev. 22:17, Mat. 6:33
and His Kingdom come to start	
Soon He'll come.....so enter the narrow gate	Lk. 21:34-36,Mat.7:13
Even though you mock me now...	II Peter 3:4
He'll come to set things straight	
Watch how I'll leave in the twinkling of an eye	I Corinthians 15:52
Don't be surprised when I go up in the sky	Revelation 3:10
There's a fire burning in my heart	Luke 24:32
Yearning for my precious Lord	Revelation 22:17
And His Kingdom come to start	Revelation 20:4-6
Your love of this world, has forsaken His	I John 2:15
It leaves me knowing that you could have had it all	Revelation 21:7
Your love of this world, was oh so reckless	Revelation 3:14-22
I can't help thinking	Philippians 1:3-6
You would have had it all	Revelation 21:7
Looking for the Son	Titus 2:13, Luke 21:36
(Tears are gonna fall, not looking for the Son)	Matthew 25:10-13
You had His holy Word in your hand	II Timothy 3:16
(You're gonna wish you had listened to me)	Jeremiah 25:4-8
And you lost it...for your self	Matthew 22:11-14
(Tears are gonna fall, not looking for the Son)	Matthew 25:10-13
Brother, I have a story to be told	Habakkuk 2:2
It's the only one that's true	John 3:16-17
And it should've made your heart turn	II Peter 3:9
Remember me when I rise up in the air	I Corinthians 15:52
Leaving your home down here	I Corinthians 15:52
For true Treasures beyond compare	Matthew 6:20
Your love of this world, has forsaken His	I John 2:15
It leaves me knowing that you could have had it all	Revelation 21:7
Your love of this world, was oh so reckless	Revelation 3:14-22
I can't help thinking	Philippians 1:3-6
You would have had it all	Revelation 21:7

(Lyrics in parentheses represent background vocals)
(CONTINUED)

Lyric	Scripture
Looking for the Son	Titus 2:13, Lk. 21:36
(Tears are gonna fall, not looking for the Son)	Matthew 25:10-13
You had His holy Word in your hand	II Timothy 3:16
(You're gonna wish you had listened to me)	Jeremiah 25:4-8
And you lost it...for your self	Matthew 22:11-14
(Tears are gonna fall, not looking for the Son)	Matthew 25:10-13
You would have had it all	Revelation 21:7
Looking for the Son	Titus 2:13, Lk. 21:36
You had His holy Word in your hand	II Timothy 3:16
But you lost it... for your self	Matthew 22:11-14

Lyric	Scripture
Lov'n the world....not the open door	I Jn. 2:15, Rev. 4:1
Down the broad way... blind to what life's really for	Matthew 7:13-14
Turn around now...while there still is time	I Jn. 1:9, II Pet. 3:9
Learn your lesson now or you'll reap just what you sow	Galatians 6:7

(You're gonna wish you had listened to me)
You would have had it all
(Tears are gonna fall, not looking for the Son)
You would have had it all
(You're gonna wish you had listened to me)
It all, it all, it all
(Tears are gonna fall, not looking for the Son)

You would have had it all
(You're gonna wish you had listened to me)
Looking for the Son
(Tears are gonna fall, not looking for the Son)
You had His holy Word in your hand
(You're gonna wish you had listened to me)
And you lost it...for your self
(Tears are gonna fall, not looking for the Son)

You would have had it all
(You're gonna wish you had listened to me)
Looking for the Son
(Tears are gonna fall, not looking for the Son)
You had His holy Word in your hand
(You're gonna wish you had listened to me)
But you lost it
You lost it
You lost it
You lost It....for your self

Scripture Summary
Jeremiah 25:4-8
Habakkuk 2:2
Matthew 6:20
Matthew 6:33
Matthew 7:13
Matthew 22:11-14
Matthew 25:10-13
Luke 21:34-36
Luke 24:332
John 3:16-17
I Corinthians 15:52
Galatians 6:7
Philippians 1:3-6
II Timothy 3:16
Titus 2:13
II Peter 3:9
II Peter 3:4
I John 1:9
I John 2:15
Revelation 3:10
Revelation 3:14-22
Revelation 4:1
Revelation 20:4-6
Revelation 21:7
Revelation 22:17

(See www.ProphecyCountdown.com for more information)

The Day of the Lord is Near!

The Coming Spiritual Earthquake

by James T. Harman

"The Message presented in this book is greatly needed to awaken believers to the false ideas many have when it comes to the Rapture. I might have titled it: THE RAPTURE EARTH-QUAKE!"
Ray Brubaker - God's News Behind the News

"If I am wrong, anyone who follows the directions given in this book will be better off spiritually. If I am right, they will be among the few to escape the great-est spiritual calamity of the ages."
Jim Harman - Author

**MUST READING FOR EVERY CHRISTIAN!
HURRY! BEFORE IT IS TOO LATE!**

www.ingramcontent.com/pod-product-compliance
Lightning Source LLC
Chambersburg PA
CBHW031521040426

42445CB00009B/340